To Paula and Alan
Good friends
Best wishes
Gregory Randall
aka
Chris Kramer.

SNOW ON THE PEA SOUP

SNOW ON THE PEA SOUP

And Other Anecdotes

GREGORY RANDALL

authorHOUSE®

AuthorHouse™ UK Ltd.
1663 Liberty Drive
Bloomington, IN 47403 USA
www.authorhouse.co.uk
Phone: 0800.197.4150

© 2013 by Gregory Randall. All rights reserved.

No part of this book may be reproduced, stored in a retrieval system, or transmitted by any means without the written permission of the author.

Published by AuthorHouse 08/27/2013

ISBN: 978-1-4918-7627-5 (sc)
ISBN: 978-1-4918-7626-8 (hc)
ISBN: 978-1-4918-7628-2 (e)

Any people depicted in stock imagery provided by Thinkstock are models, and such images are being used for illustrative purposes only. Certain stock imagery © Thinkstock.

This book is printed on acid-free paper.

Because of the dynamic nature of the Internet, any web addresses or links contained in this book may have changed since publication and may no longer be valid. The views expressed in this work are solely those of the author and do not necessarily reflect the views of the publisher, and the publisher hereby disclaims any responsibility for them.

CONTENTS

About the Author xvii

Snow on the Pea Soup (Oxford) 1

Wal! You're Eating the Doily (Australia) 1

The Rural Chicken (Norfolk, England) 2

The Cowled Monk 3

I Know Some Shortcuts! (KLM pilot) 4

"The Only Thing Today the Germans Are Not Best at Is . . ." (German banker) 4

"It's Fish or Fish on the Menu as We're . . ." (Airline) 5

There is No Such Airline as British Airways 5

A Pint of Whisky 6

Where Is Zis Londres Gatwick Anyway? 6

Missing Mount Cook (Air New Zealand) 7

Black or White Coffee Sir? (Nationalised British Railways) 9

Drones Like Me (Oxford) 9

Princess Margaret's Car (British Leyland in the 1970s) 10

The Interpretations of English Afternoon Tea (Asia) 11

I Am Sailor 13

The Japanese Concept of Fresh and the Western Concept of Dead 14

Japanese Hotels 15

Amerikya, Presidyent Clintyon (Kazakhstan) 15

The Real "Pretty Woman" Hotel 16

Oxford University—The Beginnings of My Collection of Anecdotes 17

Have a Glass of Sherry or Two—The College Principal 19

Celebrating the College's Wins at Sport by Throwing Beer Glasses 19

Academic Clerical Sense of Humour: The Knotted Sheet Rope 19

A Study of History to Encourage Thinking about a Subject
    Which Doesn't Matter 20

The Mediaeval Pornographic Novel 21

Making Sure I Didn't Work Too Hard 21

Some Thoughts on Exams 23

Military Differences 24

Different Approaches to Formality 25

Nowadays 26

The Governor of the Central Bank of Brazil and Hyperinflation 28

Polish Anti-communist Jokes 29

Bulgarian Anti-communist Joke 29

England: About Spike Milligan, Comedian 29

What's a Crèche? 30

How the Rich Live, or, More about South Kensington 30

Her Majesty On Recessions 31

Prince Andrew 31

Latin Joke 32

English Eccentricity 32

Eccentricity at a London Gentleman's Club, During the Butler's Week Off 32

The Major's Eccentricity 34

A Brace of Admirals 34

American Clubs 34

True Irish Eccentric Decisions (Not meant as jokes) 35

What Television Doesn't Reveal About the Trooping of the Colour 36

The Total Rout of Harvard MBAs by an Elderly English Gentleman 37

The Royal Egg 38

An Eccentric Building 38

An Eccentric Art Teacher 39

Travel 39

The British Embassies Abroad— 40

Best Travel Story 41

The Scariest Flights 42

Iberia Caravelle—Plane Buckets around the Sky 43

Unpleasant Flights 43

American Airlines Express (Commuter Airline to Small Cities)—
  Sludge in the Aisle 44

Aerolineas Argentinios: Not All the Flights Made It Over the South Pole 45

Singapore Airlines—Tight Skirts Around the Ankles =
  How Would They Be Able to Run in an Emergency? 45

Qantas, A Different Approach to Safety 46

Air New Zealand—A Total Failure at Controlling Very Drunk Passengers 46

Good Flights 47

Have a Drink on Us (Cyprus Airlines) 48

Thanks that this Plane Flies Itself (British Airways in Kazakhstan) 48

Difficult Airports and Aeroplanes 49

Snow and Ice 50

Concorde	50
Interesting Flights	52
The Dutch View	52
Cars	52
British Cars Before Mrs Thatcher	53
Steam from Under the Bonnet	53
Traffic Sign on Fiji	54
The Fake Maserati	55
Trains	55
The Wrong Sort of Snow	56
Lovers Train, Netherlands	57
Trains and Rural Accounting	57
Horses with Night-time Lighting	58
Tea in Harrods with Secret Agents?	59
The English Tea Habit	60
Filet Americaine	60
Is There a German Sense of Humour?	60
Most Useful Advice from an MP	61

Y vonnae vae veg (Manx Gaelic) 62

France—Vive La Difference 63

Wellington Won the Battle but Napoleon Won the War 63

The French Interpretation of the EU Human Rights Law: 64

French Unpasteurised Food 65

Luxembourg and France with Banking Secrecy 66

Why Do the French Live Much Longer Than Us? 67

French Views in Other Areas that are Radically Different from Britain's 68

French Food and a Bit of History, Too 69

French Juniper Gin 71

Actuaries and Accountants—Mathematical Geniuses at Work 72

The Actuary and the Model 72

The Actuaries and the Cannabis-Coloured Sweets from the Netherlands 73

Cambridge—An Oxford Joke 73

Actuarial Communication Skills 75

The Best Actuarial Talk 75

But Actuaries are Very Different in Brazil 76

Making Lots of Money as an Actuary 77

Accountancy Jokes 78

Prague Zoo, Czech Republic 78

The French Hot Air Balloonist 78

Australian Airport Humour 79

A Less Pleasant Arrival in Australia 80

Ayers Rock from the Air 80

Ayers Rock from the Ground 81

Japanese Tourists at the Sydney Opera House 81

Other Countries 82

Mechanical Problems 83

Islands in the Sun 83

Isle of Man 84

The Cook Islands 85

Curacao 88

Aruba 89

Cyprus 90

The Cyprus Bailout 91

Iceland 92

Malta 93

Wine 94

Chilean Wine 95

Conflict Between the Chilean and Dutch Views of Social Justice 96

Old World Wines 97

The Company Secretary of Penfolds 97

The Company Secretary of Schweppes, Australia 98

French Classified Growths—The Top of the Pyramid 98

The Chinese Influence on Wine Prices 98

Outstanding Wines 100

US Wines 100

Robert Parker 101

New World Wine Technology 101

New Zealand—Cloudy Bay Wine 102

British Airways and Wine as Compared with Some Other Airlines 103

Sauternes—Sweet Wines 104

An Unscheduled Stop—The Lesson of Buying Power 105

The Napa Valley 106

John Duval 106

White Wine 106

Canadian Ice Wine 107

Austria—The Sweet Wine Scandal 108

The Middle East 108

Banking 109

Travel 109

Carpets 110

Groceries 110

Der Cooling Down 111

Red Wine Mixed with White is the Ultimate Offence to a Winemaker 112

The Netherlands 113

Eating Habits 113

Drug Culture: Company Time and Private Time 114

The British Investment Banker and the Thirty-five Hour Week 115

Germany—The Same Idea 116

Thrift 116

The Rood Light 117

Brazil 117

Traffic and Hotels 118

Rio de Janeiro 119

Brasilia 119

Argentina 120

Russia 120

New Zealand: Lateral Thinking on the Topics of Defence and the
    Riches of the Seas 121

Sri Lanka—A Hotel's Old-Fashioned Bell Pull 123

Sweden and the Behaviour of the Japanese Royal Household 124

Italy, the Bella Signorina in the Carabinieri—Only in Italy 125

South Africa, Johannesburg Airport—The Differing Bag Count 125

The United States—Really Aggressive Airport Security Every Time 127

Most Colourful Chef 128

Work 129

My First Job Obtained by Thinking on my Feet 129

The City in the 60s—No Technology but a Place for Gentlemen 129

Bearer Shares 130

Working Conditions or Shades of Reginald Perrin (From the TV Series) 131

Stockbroking as it Was 131

Top of the Pile... 132

The Prudential Investment Department in the Early 1970s and
    Their Coat of Arms... 132

The Old Ways of Keeping Disasters Quiet. 133

Old-Fashioned Fund Management and Long Alcoholic Lunches....... 134

The Short Platform—The Really Drunk Are Truly Physically Relaxed 135

Investment in France Is Still Old-Fashioned 136

Spain.. 137

The Generalissimo Franco.. 137

The Only Banker who Understood Modern Risks................................. 138

ABN AMRO.. 139

Fred the Shred of RBS Compounds the Problem................................... 140

About the Author

I realised I looked like the author John Mortimer when people started staring at me in the National Portrait Gallery as I happened to be standing under his portrait. I am not related and have never met him. I do admire him, however, and with his televised series of his novel, *Rumpole of the Bailey*, he became widely known as a great humorous author.

My form of humour is anecdotes, which I have been collecting for over fifty years during a career which involved lots of travel on business.

I was told during my professional career that I managed to offend forty-eight nationalities in an hour's public lecture in Brussels—at least until they all realised they had heard the legendary English sense of humour.

Except for a few stories I read that are too good not be repeated, these are true anecdotes, or anecdotes told to me as true. No offence is intended. There is also the chance that my memory has sometimes failed, and I may not recount them all perfectly. Also, it should be emphasised that unless I say so (as in the Dubai anecdote), most of the stories are ten to thirty years old, and most places have changed enormously. I hope you enjoy them.

This book is dedicated to:

Carol, Barnaby, and Vicky (the talking retired alpha greyhound—a marvellous handful to live with), the key influences in my professional life.

The late Dr George Ramsay, fellow and tutor in history at St Edmund Hall, Oxford, and lecturer at Oxford University. He taught me to relax, and not to take things too seriously.

The late Norman Shepherd of Guardian Assurance Company, who taught me the basic approach to long term investment, and Investment Ethics. The latter always was a drag on my career, but at least my conscience is clear.

Dr Leonard Polonsky of Liberty Life Assurance, who gave me full reign in managing investments because "If it's working, don't fix it."

Nick Fitzpatrick of Bacon & Woodrow, Actuaries, who taught me about Investment Consulting to Pension Funds, and the relevant ethics.

I also owe a debt to Donald Duval of Hewitts, a super mathematician, actuary and Renaissance man, who really annoys me when he can out quote me in Latin.

Finally, to my two most intelligent clients—the UK Coca Cola Scheme, Belinda Brady from Atlanta, and Tina, and Malcolm from the UK; and Martyn Hurd and colleagues from The Independent Television News Pension Fund.

Snow on the Pea Soup (Oxford)

My ancient Oxford University college of St Edmund Hall had a very old dining room (now replaced by a whizz-bang model of 1960s construction). It had been built in the middle ages, and renovated in the 1660's, with very old kitchens underneath. Access from the kitchen to the dining room was via an outside staircase going out to the quadrangle then back in again. The food highlight in the winter was a hot bowl of pea soup with snow on top.

Wal! You're Eating the Doily (Australia)

The big travel agency, Trailfinders, owns a pretty remote hotel in the bush of Queensland, Australia. To get there, you have to fly to Cairns (or fly to Sydney and drive for several days, not a couple of hours as many Brits think), take a tiny plane (where passengers are given seats by their weight to ensure the plane flies evenly), then take a long drive by Land Rover, and finally a boat ride.

All the guests were British, apart from two Australians, Wally and Raylene. Wal owned a motorcycle shop in Brisbane and lived for his work. He did nothing other than fix bikes in his grease-stained overalls. However, it was their twenty-fifth wedding anniversary and Raylene was determined to get away from bikes for the weekend. Wal was a lovely man but totally lost outside of his environment. Raylene booked the special dinner for their anniversary. This was a very romantic dinner which was set up so that the couple dined in an open cabin for two by soft candlelight overlooking the rain forest and the sea.

When the happy couple got to the romantic gazebo, Wal said, "I can't see, Raylene."

"That's because it's romantic, Wal."

He said, "Oh."

Soon, the waitress arrived with the food, but after she had gone, Wal said plaintively, "This is not much dinner, Ray."

"It's only the canapés," Ray responded.

"What's that?" queried a confused Wal.

"What posh people eat before proper dinner, Wal," Ray answered patiently.

"Why?" Wal asked, continuing his confusion.

"Just eat it; you'll like it."

Well, the light from just a couple of candles wasn't very good against the total blackness of the night, and after a couple of minutes Wal said, "These canapés are a bit tough, Ray."

Ray looked closer at what Wal was eating and in quite some surprise said, "Wal! You're eating the doily."

"What's that?"

"It makes the food look nice. It goes under the canapés. And you don't eat it!"

Wal contemplated this information for a moment and stated, "I wish I had steak and chips!"

The Rural Chicken (Norfolk, England)

I am sure a lot of people living in the rural English county of Norfolk are unaware they have been members of the European Union since the 1970s, or that they are subject to a great deal of regulations from the EU. One of these that came into effect about twenty years ago was that on health and hygiene grounds, chickens could no longer be sold with their innards inside the chicken in a plastic bag.

We had a young friend and her husband staying with us who lived in London. As they hadn't much money, we took them to the local person who prepared game which had been shot locally, to be put on sale in the local butchers. He sold both of us a frozen chicken the size of a small turkey for only five pounds.

We were both going to eat our respective chickens the next night. About 6.00 p.m., we suddenly remembered our young guest might not know about the plastic bag inside the chicken containing the offal so my wife texted them in a panic, saying, "You haven't started cooking the chicken, have you?" Sure enough, she hadn't known about the custom. Our quick thinking had prevented her and her husband cooking a chicken with a plastic bag full of offal inside.

The Cowled Monk

In addition to thinking differently, the locals in Norfolk possess a dialect that lends itself to a very peculiar pronunciation.

The local church was built in 1500, replacing an earlier church from Saxon times. This was before the reformation, so there would have been monks around in their robes and hoods (known as cowls).

One day I was walking with my dog in the local churchyard when a lady came up to me and said, "It's cowled."

I immediately thought she must have seen the ghost of a monk. I couldn't see it, but said, "How wonderful to see such an apparition. Do you see ghosts here often?"

She went on to repeat, "It's cowled," louder and louder, as if I was stupid (that's another matter!).

Afterwards, I recounted the tale, and was told *cowled* was the local pronunciation of the word *cold*!

The local phrase I really like is, "I see you have the company" for "I see you have guests."

I Know Some Shortcuts! (KLM pilot)

"I'm sorry we're late taking off, but I know some shortcuts!"

"The Only Thing Today the Germans Are Not Best at Is . . ." (German banker)

When I joined a Dutch bank to work on their pensions offering, I decided to find out how Germany coped with the problems of the elderly. I found out that my German counterpart and I were born the same year, 1944.

The first time I met him, I cheerily said, "Well, I'm here because your ancestors missed, and you're here because my ancestors missed, so can we both be friends?"

He said, "Only if you now agree that Germany is best of all at the environment. In fact, Germany is the best at everything . . ." There came a slight pause, and he then offered, "Except wars—and those don't matter anymore."

That's one of the main reasons Germany is prosperous, and Britain much less so.

"It's Fish or Fish on the Menu as We're . . ." (Airline)

I was flying business class on a small airline, because it was cheaper than the British Airways economy fare.

The stewardess came round and said, "Here's the menu. Oh dear, it's not translated into English. I can tell you it's fish or fish as we're Icelandair."

Obvious when you think about it

There is No Such Airline as British Airways

Yes, this is true, and from May 2013. I was due to fly out from Dubai and wanted to check the time of my flight, since I had misplaced my itinerary. BA flies twice a day to Dubai and back from London Heathrow.

I asked my hotel concierge if she could check. She got the number for enquiries at Dubai Airport from the hotel switchboard and rang them up. She reported back to me that they had told her, "There is no such airline as British Airways." Not only that, they maintained this stance for a full five minutes. Eventually, however, they found that BA did, in fact, exist, so the concierge then informed them we needed the flight times for Flight 108. This time, Dubai Airport information replied, "There is no such flight. The only BA flight from Dubai is Flight 106 at 1:30 a.m. tomorrow morning."

Fortunately, I found my itinerary, and flew out from Dubai Airport without any problems the next morning, as arranged, on BA Flight108 at 9:30 a.m.

Memo to self, as Boris Johnson, Mayor of London, would say, "Sic transit glorias mundi." (So the glory of the world passes.)

Five hundred years of the British Empire has obviously passed into history. How much bigger is Emirates Airlines after only a few years' history than British Airways?

By the way, how did Dubai make the transition from totally bankrupt to totally solvent? Memo to David Cameron, could we please investigate merging Britain with Abu Dhabi and its oil wealth?

A Pint of Whisky

I had been to Cyprus on business, so naturally, I was travelling business class on Cyprus Airlines. I was the only passenger in business class. There were some problems with a warning light for the new Flyby Wire Airbus, which caused a delay, so the stewardess asked if I would like a drink. She was obviously on her first flight, and hailed from one of the remote villages.

I said, "I would like some whisky, please."

She looked puzzled, and looked at the drinks trolley. She found the bottle marked whisky. Knowing the British liked to drink pints of beer, she then brought me a pint of whisky.

I drank some, and fell asleep until London. But I woke up happy.

Where Is Zis Londres Gatwick Anyway?

As frequently happened, the Airtours plane returning from Tunisia had broken down. After three hours, a plane chartered from Air Liberte Algerie arrived from Algeria to take us back from whence we came.

On this replacement flight, there was free unallocated seating. I rushed for the front seat. The pilots spoke French, and so did I, to some extent. They flew with the cockpit door open in those innocent days before 9/11.

First thing I heard was one pilot saying to the other "Où se trouve ce Londres Gatwick, mon copain?" Translation: "Where is this London Gatwick anyway, my friend?" The reply was "Je ne sais pas moi non plus," or, in English, "I haven't a clue also."

The second pilot then continued, "J'ai une idée. Nous pourrions voler a travers Paris et demander où ce Londres Gatwick se trouve." (Roughly translated, "I've an idea. Let's fly over Paris and ask them.")

So, to my astonishment, we flew over Paris, they got their routing, and we arrived at Gatwick.

Our problems had not finished, though. We taxied round and round the airport, with the pilots obviously having no idea where to park. Eventually, I heard a ground controller yelling over the cockpit's radio, "No, you Algerian fools! Look for the number eight. Huit, sur le runway."

When you consider how many planes are flying, true stories like this show how resilient the systems are. No doubt Paris alerted Gatwick, and the flight was watched particularly carefully.

Missing Mount Cook (Air New Zealand)

I was travelling in an ancient propeller plane when I noticed the itinerary said, "Christchurch, Mount Cook, and Queenstown (a resort with a lake in the Southern Alps)." The stewardess announced the flight was to Queenstown, via Mount Cook.

The Captain joined in on the intercom and said, "No it isn't."

"That's the itinerary, Captain," informed the stewardess.

"But there's fog," responded the Captain, "and I can't see it, we've no instruments for this, and I'm in charge."

On the way back, the flight to Mount Cook was uneventful. From Queenstown there was only me, a rugby player and the stewardess in the cabin. The stewardess was intent on talking to the rugby player, who certainly had a lot of muscles, so I was left alone. I imagined that Mount Cook airport had a flat field. Not so! It was at the foot of a mountain, surrounded by huge glacial boulders.

At Mount Cook airport, a busload of Japanese tourists boarded the plane. The rugby player and I were on the left side, and all the Japanese were on the right. The Japanese tour director asked the stewardess if some of them could move to the left side.

The stewardess answered, "No."

Surprised by this, the tour director asked why not.

She answered rather laconically, "Because you're on the right for a reason."

The flight then took off and, in order to miss hitting the mountain, it immediately banked to 45 degrees. The weight of the Japanese all being on the right, helped to balance the plane.

By the way, the South Island of New Zealand is uncompromisingly rural. It is the size of England, has a population of five hundred thousand people in addition to sixty million sheep. This works out to one one sheep per acre. It has a really laid back rural accent. For instance, I am told the following words are pronounced the same in the local accent: six, socks, sacks, and sex. There is a joke about that, but I've forgotten it.

Black or White Coffee Sir? (Nationalised British Railways)

In the time before the privatisation of British Railways, I had an experience where the steward walked through my carriage carrying two large coffee pots. He enquired of me, "Black or white, Sir?"

I responded with, "Black, please."

To which he said, "Er, they're both already mixed."

Drones Like Me (Oxford)

When the results of my final exams were known, my tutor (professor) needed to write to me.

For reasons known only to ancient history (I would guess Eleanor of Aquitaine had something to do with it, since she seemed to have been behind many complicated historical events), Oxford was the only university which did not separate second class honours into 2:1 and 2:2. Some jobs, such as the higher grades of the Civil Service, and degrees like the Doctorate of Philosophy (shortened to D.Phil in Oxford, but PhD in newer universities like Cambridge) required at least a 2:1 as an academic qualification.

Thus, the need for a letter from your tutor at Oxford, which you could show if needed. Both of my best friends were going to do D.Phils, and both eventually became lecturers at other ancient universities—one at Durham and the other at St Andrews.

My tutor wrote something like this to me:

"I am pleased to say that, had the second class been divided, you would have been placed in the upper half. I know you have no interest in the Civil Service. (Was this because to a nineteen-year-old the recruiting talk for the Civil Service was about the work of a Principal at the Home Office on how thrilling it was to chair the middle two years of the expected six for the panel on re-drafting the law on coroners and death certificates?)

I know you have some interest in a D.Phil. In your case, although I cannot stopyou, I would not recommend this course of action. I believe you are one of my rare students who could make a living in the field of commerce. I am not exactly sure what commerce is. However, I know we need graduates to go into it, because it provides taxes which support drones like me."

What a wonderfully realistic attitude, to be contrasted with university lecturers today, who often scorn the very means of making the money which pays them. To its eternal shame, Oxford voted against giving Lady Thatcher an honorary degree. Without her, Britain today would have an equivalent standard of living to Cuba.

Princess Margaret's Car (British Leyland in the 1970s)

British cars, until Mrs Thatcher abolished exchange controls, were of a terrible standard. This was due to the fact that foreign currency was not available to buy foreign cars, so there was no competition. Applying mahogany veneer was the excuse for spending nothing on engineering.

The Royal family were not exempt. Princess Margaret, the Queen's sister, had a square-looking Rover car. After she had returned the vehicle as not working to her garage three times in one month, she invoked privilege, and sent it back to the Rover factory with instructions not to send it back until it was mended properly.

The car was put just inside the main gates with a notice saying it was Princess Margaret's car, and could we fix it properly, chaps.

Well they did. By the end of the day every bit of the car had been stolen, and passed over the wall for resale by the workers.

The only thing left were the number plates. In those days, management had to be innovative. So, they fixed the number plates onto a new car of the same colour and sent it back to Princess Margaret.

She wrote back to British Leyland, who, at the time, owned Rover, saying, "I knew you could fix the car if you tried properly."

The Interpretations of English Afternoon Tea (Asia)

English afternoon tea was immortalised in poetry. Rupert Brooke, a soldier killed in the First World War, wrote nostalgically of Grantchester from the trenches.

Stands the clock at ten to three.

And is there honey still for tea?

I went to the old rectory in Grantchester for tea decades ago. The church clock was stopped at ten to three. The tea was fine, but I still don't see how honey is involved with the traditional English afternoon tea.

Two places in London, Fortnum and Mason and the Ritz, are famous enough to have published books on the subject.

When I had tea at Fortnum and Mason, they tried hard but fell victim to using foreign staff, unaccustomed to English cooking. They offered Welsh Rarebit (toast, with a sauce consisting of melted Cheddar Cheese, beer and mustard), served after after the cakes.

I give them lots of marks for this traditional savoury. However, I asked the nice German waiter for Worcestershire sauce. This is traditionally dripped over Welsh Rarebit, to provide a bit of spice. The waiter couldn't make out what I wanted, so I wrote it down. The kitchen decanted it into a jug instead of sending the bottle. This meant there was no drip nozzle, and the Worcester sauce flooded the Rarebit, spoiling it.

The Ritz was fine, but it gave a real production line feel in terms of the amount of persons served per hour.

At the Ritz Carlton in Bahrain they tried, but the Asian head waitress on duty at the advertised "English Afternoon Tea" was totally surprised that tea involved milk in any way.

The real disappointment was the Oriental in Bangkok. The legendary hotel has rooms that are somewhat dated, and even the view of the wonderful river can now be found at more modern hotels. The appeal, I would say, is the tiny hotel from the 1930s which is attached to the modern hotel. Here, many authors, such as Conrad and Graham Greene, sat and wrote novels alongside the great slow, wide river Chao Pharya which runs through the centre of Bankgkok. Indeed, the most modern writer to do so was Geoffrey Archer. He opened a library of books which had been written at the hotel. A small brass plaque was put up to commemorate the opening. My next visit happened to be after he had gone to prison. The plaque had been removed, but there were still four tiny screw holes in the mahogany panelling.

Anyway, the tea was an Asian version of the original. The waitresses were far too pushy, terrorising the mainly Japanese guests. First, the tea was brought and poured straight into the cup. The waitresses were unaware that many British tea drinkers take their milk first.

An Oxford contemporary, who was completing a chemistry D.Phil, experimented, and found that pouring the tea onto the milk or the milk onto the tea affected the way the proteins in the milk curdled. So, it wasn't just imagination that the tea tasted different.

Secondly, scones should be served when diners have finished their sandwiches, but before cake. Instead, they were served for the convenience of the waitresses, which was when the scones were ready. I did not take well to my scones being served with a snapped, "Eat them now, they're hot," from the waitress, while I was still eating my sandwiches. I didn't bother to try to teach the lazy servers either some elementary manners or the rules of English tea.

This is from Thailand, a nation which holds dear its custom of bowing.

I Am Sailor

A dinner meeting was arranged in order to discuss the potential takeover of my then-employer by a French life company. Naturally, this was held at a French restaurant in London at 1.00 a.m. Only beef was served, which I considered completely uncooked based on the amount of red blood. However, the French liked the dish.

The Frenchman I was sitting next to said, "Hello. I am Sailor."

I was then forced to reply, "Hello, Sailor."

He then added, "I am Sailor Man."

It took me a few minutes to work out he was their Marketing Director.

The Japanese Concept of Fresh and the Western Concept of Dead

I am allergic to shellfish and the allergy increases with the thickness of the shell. Therefore, lobster is something I don't even contemplate including in my diet. I don't even like looking at it, particularly when it is alive. However, my colleague liked lobster.

On a business trip to Tokyo one time, we were taken to a Teppanyaki grill by some Japanese suppliers. The Teppanyaki grill is a hot metal cooking surface which diners sit around. Usually the chefs are proficient at wielding various knives, and may even throw them around the grill.

Meat is cut into small squares and grilled, and is very nice. But my colleague and the two Japanese businessmen that accompanied us that evening, had asked for lobster. I wondered what was going on when three brass domes were brought.

Don't read on if you're squeamish.

The chef took three live lobsters and put them onto the very hot grill. To say the least, they wriggled. He sliced each of them in half lengthwise. He then put the brass domes over them. Noticing no domes for the lobsters at the next grill, we asked the Japanese businessmen why. They said the domes were only used when westerners were dining, because it had been discovered the Japanese concept of fresh and the western concept of dead did not meet in the middle for eating lobster.

Luckily, I had ordered steak and have never enjoyed it more.

Japanese Hotels

I visited Japan quite a lot on business. Yet, I never really understood the enormous cultural differences. We stayed in the Okura Hotel because it was next to my company's office, and it was possible to walk to and from without getting lost.

I, therefore, joined the Okura Club, which is similar to that of many hotel chains. The difference was in the benefits. One of which, as far as I could see, allowed that I could have two shirts laundered free of charge. As well, every time I checked in, the concierge would shout "Okura Crubu". This would cause all employees present in the lobby to bow at me. The bellboy would then run my bag up to my room, and then hide around the corner until I had entered. He could then knock and be able to say, "So sorry to be late."

Similarly, the lift was modernised. I found this unfortunate, because previously, there had been a wonderful lady in full dress kimono to press the buttons on the lift. Strangely, after modernisation, she was still there, but only to greet guests as they entered and to gesture that they had to press their own buttons. Of course, if guests did nothing, she would press the button for them, as before.

Amerikya, Presidyent Clintyon (Kazakhstan)

In my capacity as Money Purchase pension adviser to a big Dutch Bank, I was volunteered to be in charge, amongst many other things, of our operation in Kazakhstan. The importance of Kazakhstan was that it contains what are probably the world's largest oil reserves, under the Caspian Sea—with only one major problem, which is politically how to get the oil to the sea somewhere. For a Bank, an early presence in this country was getting in on the ground floor of revenues which would consequently result in a very big oil reserve fund.

I was speaking to the Minister for Pensions, Civil Defence, and Protection of the Constitution. Presumably, he had been given the Ministries which weren't very important. (We could do well to follow this brilliant idea, which would cut the amount of civil servants enormously.)

I had spoken for half an hour, including the time it took for the translation into Russian.

Throughout my speech, the Minister had stoically read Pravda, the popular Russian Communist Party national newspaper, instead of appearing to listen to my words.

As we were leaving he began speaking in English and I wondered what was going to happen.

He said "Americya. Presidyent Clintyon. Monica Lewinsky."

I wondered even more what he was going to say next. But, I didn't have to wait long before he continued with, "Too much democracy."

I believe she certainly wouldn't have tried it on in Kazakhstan.

Incidentally, we spend too much time criticising countries like Kazakhstan, without being mindful of how recently they were communist dictatorships. Even as an occasional visitor, progress was visible.

And Other Anecdotes

The Real "Pretty Woman" Hotel

I was on business in Los Angeles and I had a free morning, so I went to the centre of Hollywood. I noticed I was passing the Beverly

Wiltshire hotel, which I had heard was used for the filming of Pretty Woman. The reception area was just as it appeared in the film.

To me the main feature of the hotel in the film was the perfect staff. No English butler could be more discreet and professional. I decided to test this by taking coffee, and seeing if the real staff were as legendary as their fictional selves.

I walked into the dining room as a casual guest, wearing a blazer, which is very formal by California standards.

I sat down and a minute later a waiter, who looked more like an English butler, arrived to take my order. He put a folded, ironed, Wall Street Journal, on my side plate. I ordered coffee and a pastry in my English accent. A minute later the butler silently removed the Wall Street Journal, and substituted an ironed, folded, Financial Times.

However, perfection does not last. A few years later, I stayed for the night and I found that the hotel had changed hands. I asked for table for dinner, and was told they now had a designer restaurant with a famous chef, and it was fully booked. I asked if they kept a free table for potential hotel guests until mid-evening, like many upmarket hotels. Clearly their designer restaurant was too profitable for that.

Sad, but obvious, that the desire to increase profits should affect service at one of the world's best hotels. No doubt the hotel or its management style will have changed frequently since then.

Oxford University—The Beginnings of My Collection of Anecdotes

I was born at the end of the war. There was not much fun to be had in the 1940s and '50s, with food rationing still in force; therefore, it is my opinion that nostalgia is inappropriate. The overall standard of living was pretty basic. However I was lucky enough to gain admission to the Oxford University College, St Edmund Hall. In 1963, this was the last refuge of the concept that an Oxbridge education is not just academic, but also to develop character.

(Please differentiate this from the rather silly goings on of rich undergraduates, such as the Bullingdon club. St Edmund Hall was for people from ordinary backgrounds.)

To save confusion, Oxford is a collegiate university. You join a college of the university. It gives accommodation, usually for the first year only, as well as tuition in your subject. A number of university lecturers are elected as fellows of colleges, where they give these tutorials. These tutorials are given to usually only two undergraduates at a time, and only once a week. There are also university lectures and laboratories. In my day, colleges held their own entrance exams, but all the other exams were given by the university.

The Entrance Interview for St Edmund Hall, Originally a Monastic Teaching Hall, and the Oldest College: The Test of the Rugby Ball.

To my view, the entrance interview went very well, since I got the two history tutors arguing.

At the end of the interview, the Principal gave me the legendary sporting test. I was given a rugby ball and told to throw it over the Principal's desk into his waste paper bin. I missed by a mile. I was asked if my missing the goal was deliberate and I replied, "No, I have no interest in sport."

I went away thinking that I had just interviewed at a great sporting college, therefore, I had failed. I did not know that the college took on new students at a ratio of 50 per cent with an inclination toward sport (many of whom went on to represent their country), and 50 per cent non-sport directed to make the sportsmen work harder. Therefore, I had passed!

Have a Glass of Sherry or Two—The College Principal

My first term started with the Principal's sherry party. I was exhorted to, "Have a glass of sherry or two, but not both at once."

The Principal was an austere-seeming clergyman and a world expert at some part of the Bible specific to the Middle Ages. Underneath that public personality was a man who, whenever the college won a sporting cup (which was frequently), could down a bottle of wine in a couple of minutes and sing rugby songs with the best of them.

Celebrating the College's Wins at Sport by Throwing Beer Glasses

These sporting successes brought their own tradition of drinking in celebration. At some stage, the athletes concerned and their friends decided the best way to complete their celebrations would be to throw their empty beer glasses over the roof of the eighteenth century chapel, into the teaching fellow's garden at New College next door. However, their tutors were pretty humourless, and the practice was eventually stopped.

Academic Clerical Sense of Humour: The Knotted Sheet Rope

The Dean, who was another clergyman, had responsibility for college discipline, such as it was. The Rev Dr Graham Midgley had a dry sense of humour. The college gates were still locked at midnight, and all students were supposed to be in college by then.

The Dean's accommodation was in a building overlooking the High Street. In the early hours of one morning, he looked out of his window and saw a rope of knotted sheets attached to the outside of the window of the room next door.

Using his pass key, he entered the room, and collected the sheet rope. He then attached this to his own window and waited. Around dawn, one at a time, all the members of the rugby football first fifteen, unsuspectingly, climbed up the rope into what they thought was one of their rooms. Instead, they found the Dean waiting. He fined each of them five pounds for college funds on the spot—a lot of money at the time!

A Study of History to Encourage Thinking about a Subject Which Doesn't Matter

The study of history has always been, in my opinion, an excellent way to develop logical thought about things which don't matter.

For example, one paper containing two compulsory statements requiring essay, before the days of multiple choice. The first compulsory statement was "King John was a bad King. Discuss." The second was "King John was a good King. Discuss." This examined the students' ability to develop logical thought without prejudice, because the answer didn't matter.

My first tutorial paper was torn to bits academically. For my second paper, I found an article on the subject that my tutor had not included in my reading list. I wrote down those arguments as my next weekly essay, and presented it at my second tutorial.

I was surprised when it, too, was torn to bits. I enquired as to why, since it was his argument. He said the purpose of the education was to learn to argue, and take all aspects into consideration. That was the advantage of history. The answers do not matter, only the way of approaching them does.

The Mediaeval Pornographic Novel

The real difference with an Oxford education is that it is based on a weekly tutorial where, for an hour, two students present essays and discuss them with a tutor who is a college fellow (professor).

Dr Ramsey, my history tutor, and author of the famous historical research paper, "Wiltshire Woollen Industry in the Sixteenth and Seventeenth Centuries" (one of the first works of historical research concentrating on the common people rather than Kings and Queens), had a good sense of humour.

For my third tutorial, there was a huge reading list. I was already developing a method of speed reading the introduction of a book as well as its conclusion, and dipping into bits which looked interesting. So I quickly ploughed through the list. The second-to-last book was a mediaeval racy novel, printed on purple paper. At the next tutorial, I asked what it was for and was told, "It is to see how many get to that stage in the reading list."

Making Sure I Didn't Work Too Hard

My tutor had seen me coming out of the Bodleian Library on a Saturday morning in my first term and took the view I was clearly working too hard. I understand he had told my friends they should get me drunk since that was a more suitable occupation for the first year student.

Upon hearing this I queried, "Why then do you arrange your university lectures to begin at 8.00 a.m. on Saturdays?"

My tutor replied, "Because if fewer than eight people attend each of the first three of your lecture series, a university lecturer can discontinue the series of lectures and still get paid!"

I think by that time St Edmund Hall was probably the last remnant of Oxford education which took the view that university was there to develop personalities, rather than just intensive study. This method still produced good academic results, however. National Service had just finished and the college had decided that eighteen-year-olds coming straight from school were too immature to benefit from this, and they didn't admit anyone under nineteen. I sometimes wonder what the occasional teenage maths genius gets out of university, since maths is a subject where what matters is the right answer, not its interpretation.

The extent to which the modern university of Oxford is different is conting petty interference from governments. On the one hand Qxford is one of only two European universities in the top ten. It does world class research. For example, the Princial of St Edmund Hall is also a university professor, heading a department researching malaria, for the benefit of the poorest countries of Africa

None of Oxford's American competitors has to put up with the mindless interference of the Education Ministry in England. As an example, there is a televised murder mystery series, Inspector Morse, which happens to be set in Oxford. Apparently, some school pupils think a series with several murders a day is real, so won't apply to Oxford University for fear of being murdered. Instead of putting these pupils who cannot distinguish fact from obvious fiction into remedial school, Oxford is being made to waste its precious money and resources teaching these pupils that Morse is fiction.

How does this come about in England? It can't be the minister, Mr Gove, as I am told he has no ideas. At one stage he was a junior reporter for Independent Television News (ITN). A cameraman I know says Gove was so unremarkable that he had been gone for a year before anybody realised he was gone. Therefore, it has to be the policy of his left wing civil servants. His Sir Humphrey, Permanent Secretary, must still be a Communist, red in tooth and claw.

England's big problem is these permanent civil servants are unsackable. Why not make him ambassador to Cuba? A friend went on holiday to Cuba, and saw on her last day there was an elderly man gardening outside her room. All she had left was a quarter of a tube of English toothpaste. She gave it, with apologies, to the gardener. He broke down in tears at her generosity. Sir Humphrey would do well there, and the foreign office could stop sending the embassy food parcels.

Some Thoughts on Exams

Nowadays there are a lot of adverse comments on exams. If anything, there was more to criticise in my day. My A Level geography paper was sharply marked down by an external examiner from another county because I did not quote from my county's volume of the standard geography of England. Later, I discovered this was due to the fact that it had not been published, and it was the examiner who was ignorant, not I.

In my day, Oxford colleges had their own entrance exams and interviews. My first attempt was at University College, which was subsequently attended by Chelsea Clinton. One examiner was asleep on a sofa throughout the interview. I failed.

My then-current school was surprised by this and wrote University College to ask why. University College replied that I had failed because my Latin paper was so bad. Presumably this was written by the tutor who was asleep during the interview. My school replied back with the unarguable fact that I hadn't done a Latin paper. University College's rebuttal was something along the lines of: "Well, he failed anyway."

If that had been Chelsea Clinton, there would have been the diplomatic row to end all rows.

Military Differences

Le Plus ca Change, le Plus, C'est la Même Chose!

(The More It Changes, the More It Is the Same Thing!)

I'm not sure exactly what this means, but NATO armies are all trying to do the same thing, But the way they do it is very different. In the United States, the commercial sector does most of the work on new equipment. Therefore, it works.

In Britain, the work is done by the Ministry of Defence's civil servants, who have never probably worked in industry. They detest giving preference to the best firm, yet their technical qualifications are probably in Greek and Latin.

By the cold war, this had caused Britain to become the laughing stock of Europe. There is a story of a US NATO general watching tank exercises out on the German plain. There was the whine of gas turbines, and a number of bushes with US Abrams tanks underneath them moved forward. There was the gentle hum of Mercedes diesel engines, and more bushes with German Leopard tanks underneath them moved forward. There was a great smell of garlic (my pathetic joke) and bushes with French Leclerc tanks underneath them moved forward quietly, on their fuel of smally cheese and wine.

Finally, there was an ear-splitting noise which went on for ten minutes accompanied by masses of black smoke from the remaining bushes, and then nothing. The British tanks wouldn't move.

Even worse than this, as inflation fell throughout the 1980s, and the cost of electronic components went into free fall, the Ministry of Defence's civil servants were congratulated by Parliament for having put in fixed price contracts for electronic components. You don't want to know how much this cost, or that it took about a decade for the civil servants to realise.

Different Approaches to Formality

British soldiers love dressing up in fancy uniforms. There is probably not much harm in it, since they currently all have to serve in Afghanistan.

A NATO commander was retiring, and wished to inspect all the troops on duty at NATO headquarters. The sound of, "Éēn, twee, drie" could be heard coming from a drill sergeant as the Dutch conscripts shuffled past. Then, there came the sound of marching music from fife and drums, and the British contingent, which happened to be from The Grenadier Guards, marched past perfectly in their red uniforms, complete with Bearskins.

My good friend Jack, now retired and living in Phoenix, Arizona, was a Major in the US National Guard Air Force at the time of the first Gulf War. He commanded a wing of thirty-six air tankers, comprising his own Philadelphia National Guard, the Tennessee National Guard, and the Mountain Men of one of the North West states.

At the time, his part of the US National Guard Air Force was sent to Dubai for the first Gulf War. The ground logistics in Dubai were looked after by the UK Royal Air Force. Food was a very important part of the ground logistics and I believe that if it had been the US Air Force in charge, it would have been cold pizza on the plane and hot pizza from a buffet on arrival. However, my friend was met on arrival in Dubai by a senior RAF officer who asked if he had his dress uniform with him.

Fortunately, it was always on his plane, although as National Guard, he never wore it. Preparing himself thusly, and upon entering the dinner, he found to his shock that as far as the RAF were concerned, dinner meant silver service with ground airmen as servants.

On a lighter note, the good people of Philadelphia sent a pallet of Heinz sauces, made in that city. Not to be outdone, the good people of Tennessee sent a pallet of Jim Beam. Unsurprisingly, the Jim Beam quickly disappeared before making it tothe National Guard of Tennessee. I would imagine the customs officer who made it disappear is still passed out on a beach in Dubai.

It takes a particularly calm temperament to fly tankers in a war zone.

Congratulations on your retirement, Jack.

Nowadays

Britain has now manufactured a fine tank, just as tanks are not needed.

However, there has been a major change. Historically, all British Defence secretaries have wanted to be Generals or Admirals. The present secretary got his job after his predecessor had to resign and is now an accountant. He is therefore the first Defence Secretary familiar with accounting.

For the first time, the Generals have been rumbled. The current secretary recently announced that he had discovered the British Army had more horses (500) than tanks (350). The justification in economic terms for all the horses, replete with the pomp and ceremony that goes along with them, is not defence, but tourism. So many tourists love the Changing of the Guard that, in my opinion, it is high time this activity (given they all also serve in Afghanistan from time to time) of the British Army was put on the tourism budget. In that way, it could be expanded with even more of the splendid displays from the army.

It is really very encouraging that army procurement is to be outsourced to the private sector and no longer the domain of the civil servant, since they have shown they do not understand commerce.

I am optimistic that, provided the government does not change, this will all change in the future.

Finally, not many people know that the last real cavalry action took place during the Boer war in South Africa at the end of the nineteenth century. The Boers were Dutch farmers who outrode all the posh British cavalry regiments, because they were farmers and could ride for days. They were defeated by the British Yeomanry, which nowadays we would call Territorial Army or National Guard, because they were also farmers and could use the same tactics. My great grandfather was in the Cheshire Yeomanry; but, when I worked in England for a South African company, I thought it was wise not to tell them.

The biggest shambles of a military parade.

A few years ago, we were in Strasbourg, in France, on Bastille day. There are military parades on Bastille day. In Britain, these are planned by the military, and the town hall clears the route. In France, the town hall, or Mairie, has total control of everthing in the town. Thus some arrogant female fonctionnaire, who had not done military service, had obviously been in total charge of the parade.

I looked at the parade formed up ready to march and fell about laughing. Shortly afterwards, the bugles sounded, and the quick march was played.

The problem was, the organiser had put a dozen French Foreign legionnaires in the middle of ordinary infantry. The legionnaires are very big. They also only slow march, accompanied by their marching chant. They are not taught the quick march and cannot do it. Therefore, the legionnaires slow marched, with the other troops around them quick marching. The other troops fell over the legionnaires, who were built like rocks.

Afterwards, a French lady apologised to us saying their troops were so dreadful compared with English Parades. I said "ah, it's all in the organisation, realising that in the French system nobody would dare to blame the lady from the Mairie.

Some Traditional Anecdotes Which Ought to be True but Probably Aren't

I can't avoid telling some of the best anecdotes I've heard. If they are not true, they so illustrate the truth they should have been true.

The Governor of the Central Bank of Brazil and Hyperinflation

These two stories come from the time of hyperinflation, when inflation in Brazil was running at over 25 per cent per month (compared with the peak in Britain in the 1970s of about 25 per cent per annum). I was given a 500,000 Cruzeiro note when its value had fallen to the equivalent of one-quarter penny in sterling.

A US journalist asked the Governor of the Brazilian Central Bank, "What is the value of Brazil's debt?" The Governor answers in trillions of dollars. The journalist then clarifies, "I meant in Cruzeiros." The Governor took a bit of time to think and replied, "I must think, as I've never been asked that . . . I don't know . . . I suppose all of them."

The Governor was asked to clarify why no Brazilian citizen may be in possession of more than fifty US dollars in foreign currency. The Governor was able to answer the query with, "Well, Brazil is a very important country. It is consulted by the IMF, etc. So, it is not appropriate for any individual to have more foreign exchange than the Central Bank has."

Polish Anti-communist Jokes

These two jokes date from the time of communism in Poland.

There is a huge wedding cake-style building which towers over Warsaw and was gift from Stalin. Why were the front steps of this building the favourite place in Warsaw for lovers to meet? Answer: because it's the only place in Warsaw from which you can't see the Stalin tower.

Why do Polish police cars always contain three policemen? Because one can read, the second can write, and the third is a political commissar to keep an eye on the two intellectuals.

Bulgarian Anti-communist Joke

First comrade: "Our potato harvest is so big this year that it would stretch from Bulgaria to the feet of God."

Second comrade: "But in Bulgaria we don't believe in God."

First comrade: "And in Bulgaria we don't believe we have any potatoes either."

England: About Spike Milligan, Comedian

He was born in British India, and had lost his parents' birth certificates, and he never had one. Despite being one of our best known comedians, someone in the Home Office, without a sense of humour, decided that meant he had to be deported to back to India, when he was quite old.

Of course Spike became desperate and decided to find a solution to this problem. He rang the Irish Embassy in London and after his explanation of his situation, a man on the phone said, "Ah, are you the famous Mr Millington that's on the television?" Spike answered yes. The man then says, "You must be Irish because you are very funny, and we Irish all have a good sense of humour. Besides, there are only three million of us in Ireland, so we could do with a few more." And he processed the Irish passport for Spike.

When Spike died, he wanted the following inscribed on his tombstone: "I told you I was ill." However, the relevant priest refused. Eventually, he was forced into a compromise, and the epitaph was put on Spike's grave in Latin.

What's a Crèche?

I don't mean the obvious answer of a kindergarten. I mean an accident between two cars in South Kensington (where Princess Di taught.)

How the Rich Live, or, More about South Kensington

A lady in South Kensington was driving her Range Rover very carefully as she wanted to park in a small space for the size of her car. Driving by the book, she pulled alongside and ahead of the space in order to parallel park

Suddenly, a Mini Cooper moving quickly, whipped into the space just behind her as she was beginning her manoeuvres. The cheeky youth in the Mini then got out, and shouted, "That's what you can do if you're very young and very cheeky, Mrs."

The lady driver put her foot on the accelerator, and crashed backwards into the Mini, wrecking it. This was during the time when Range Rovers had a solid steel undercarriage, made from girders.

She got out of her vehicle and stated, "My Man, that's what you can do when you are very old and very rich."

Her Majesty On Recessions

"One knows about recessions because one has experienced them before. What one does not know, is why one's Prime Ministers never know what to do about them."

Sources tell me this is not true, but it should be because it gives a true sense of the length of her reign. I forget how many American presidents it equals.

The degree to which her Majesty knows what is going on is illustrated during a televised visit to the Bank of England. On seeing the gold, she said something like, "I understand there's rather less of it than there used to be?" This showed she was aware Gordon Brown, the Prime Minister who was never elected, squandered Britain's assets, which included selling most of our gold reserves just before the price of gold went through the stratosphere.

Prince Andrew

My personal experience of the Royal family at work in the early 1980s lies with Prince Andrew. My department had booked a function room for our Christmas party. Next door there was a similar room with very loud noises coming from it and a couple of men in suits outside the door, who told us to clear off when we got too near. Young ladies staggered out of the room to visit the loo, talking in piercing upper class accents.

Eventually one, even drunker than the others, staggered into our room and said, "Excuse me, which is the door to Prince Andrew's party?"

Latin Joke

"Caesar aderat forte, sed Brutus adsum jam."

Try pronouncing it! It's genuine and translated roughly means that Caesar is coming as fast as he can, but Brutus is already here.

English Eccentricity

Like humour, eccentricity is dying out in England, Maybe it's because life has become too money orientated. Eccentricity was common in England amongst the upper classes, but has now almost died out. That's a pity because I believe it enriched the quality of life and as a happy consequence—puzzled foreigners. Eccentricity is closely linked with the English sense of humour.

Eccentricity at a London Gentleman's Club, During the Butler's Week Off

Some years ago I used to occasionally go to a club in St James's Square in London for lunch. There was a round table for members eating on their own. One Monday, the usual Colonel was presiding and he didn't know that it was the butler's week off. The club had sourced a temporary butler, who was a French lady. There was total incomprehension between her and the Colonel.

She asked him, "What would you like for lunch, mon Colonel?"

He waved the menu away, as he always did, with an "Ah, nothing on the menu. I'll have my usual light lunch." Unfortunately the French lady had not been briefed as to what that might have been, so she took a guess at what he meant by light lunch, and replied "Maybe a light salad?"

Now, the Colonel had absolutely no idea what a salad was, and had never even seen one. But, he replied, "Well yes, I suppose so."

The lady duly brought his salad. The Colonel looked at the plate in astonishment, poked the food warily with his knife and fork, and said, "But where's the meat?" This was meant literally, not figuratively, like Ronald Reagan to a political opponent.

The waitress, still confused by what an English Colonel meant by a light lunch, asked, "Maybe you do not like this and I can bring something else?"

The Colonel had the English don't make a fuss characteristic, so he managed to push the salad round the plate, and later went nearby to the Dog and Duck pub for his usual light lunch of steak and kidney pudding (the one where the outside is made from suet/animal fat) and roast potatoes with no vegetables.

I must say, I agree with the Colonel that salad is for rabbits. I saw a young chap in my office eating a salad once. It turned out that his fiancée, being British of Chinese origin, could be very fierce and was making him lose weight.

I said, "Put the salad in somebody else's waste paper basket, and come out with me for a proper bloke's lunch of steak and chips."

Showing a decided lack of moral fibre, so prevalent in young people today, he instead told her what my suggestion had been. It wasn't long before she came round and reminded me she was captain of the ladies football team, and her boots had studs in them. Sometimes I wonder about the younger generation.

The Major's Eccentricity

And while we're on the subject of eccentricity: Meanwhile, the Major next to the Colonel, considered that plastic seals on wine bottles were hugely improper compared with the old lead seals. He ordered his normal half bottle of club claret, and the wine waiter's penknife. He, as always, used the knife to shred the plastic seal all over the floor of the dining room, and then allowed the wine waiter to open the bottle, eliminating the chance of plastic getting into the wine.

A Brace of Admirals

I don't know the proper terminology for a group of Admirals, but I saw them in the evening at this same club. They were all wearing dress spurs. I cannot imagine what the connection is between commanding an aircraft carrier and riding a horse. However, the cavalry have their own traditions.

When the new barracks was built for the Household Cavalry in Hyde Park, it was two stories high, with the officers' Dining Mess on the second floor. The officers said that wouldn't do at all. At celebratory dinners they are joined by their horses, which would be unable to get into the lift.

American Clubs

Some years back, I was invited to lunch in a club in Chicago and what impressed me most was a lady member coming in with a baby in a pushchair, and giving both to the Maître d'. He was Italian and handled the baby in a wonderful manner. I accept this might be American eccentricity, or maybe it's just normal.

True Irish Eccentric Decisions (Not meant as jokes)

I once visited the Republic of Ireland in the 1970s. As I was representing an enormous foreign investment fund, I got the top tier treatment. The economic solutions were brilliant insomuch as they were unexpected.

I was with a minister when a civil servant came in and said, "Sir. Sir. This well that BP is drilling off Cork . . ."

"Ah," said the minister, "that well is a good thing."

"Well, said the civil servant, they've just said there's no oil there."

The minister, without hesitating, said "Well, tell them to look again."

A few months before I visited, the Irish had given up the British pound in favour of their own currency, the Punt. The most effective decision was when another civil servant came in and said, "Sir. Sir. This American Bank is shorting the Punt."

"What does that mean?" said the minister.

"It means they're-selling our currency which they don't have, and forcing down its value, so things become more expensive here."

"Ah," replied the minister, "that would be a bad thing. Who has got the Punts?"

The civil servant replied, "Well, since the currency's new, 90 per cent of it is still at our local banks."

"Well," said the minister, "tell our banks not to give these Americans any of our currency."

This lateral thinking decision blindsided the American bank, because they couldn't close their short position until they apologised to the Irish Government.

I would like to say they never did it again, but by the mid-1980s they had forgotten. They shorted the Kiwi, or New Zealand dollar. The amount in circulation is tiny, because New Zealand is a small country, doing all its trade in strong currencies.

A friend, who lived in Hong Kong, had, as a sole trader, cornered the small free market in the Kiwi dollar for many years. When the American bank found out, they asked if they could borrow some Kiwis to close their short. My friend said no.

What Television Doesn't Reveal About the Trooping of the Colour

In the innocent 1960s, I was walking through the Horse Guards Parade yard, when I saw a notice posted near some stands "Rehearsal for the Trooping of the Colour. Please join us." So I did. Nowadays, I would have to have applied weeks in advance, be security vetted, and go through a metal detector.

The thing that does not come through televisions, obviously, is the overwhelming smell after the horses of the Household Cavalry ride past; nor the fact that after they pass, the foot guards don't go bang bang with their feet, but squish squish.

The Total Rout of Harvard MBAs by an Elderly English Gentleman

When I worked as head of research for a stock broker in the North of England during the early 1970s, there was a nice, chap, who was elderly by then, and was a well-known countryman. He was very upper class and clearly very intelligent. As well, he wrote a column for *Field* magazine that was totally self-parodying and he would write such things as, "My weary horse knew his own way home," etc. However, he had the upper class characteristic of minimising his intelligence in public.

Aged about 40, he had become Managing Director of Andrews Liver Salts in the small Northumberland town of Morpeth. The US company, Sterling Winthrop, decided to bid for Andrews Liver Salts. At the time, MBAs in business were then the rage and several were sent to Morpeth.

The company showed to have fine credibility, and the US CEO asked the MBAs if there would be any problem getting rid of the management? They replied something along the lines of, "No problem. The only one who matters is an ancient Brit who can't even string a sentence together."

So they fired Henry, the "ancient Brit" and discovered the hard way that he was the first person in Britain who had an unbreakable service contract for life. He took Sterling Winthrop to court and won an amazing amount in damages. He retired at forty, and measured out his retirement in things which gave him pleasure, such as visiting the rural hills, and gaining a little income by taking stockbroking orders from the tiny rural banks. He continued this for years and years

The Royal Egg

Her Majesty is legendary for her admirable frugality. She is supposed to use the back of old envelopes for notes to avoid buying Post It notes. Another example is that Her Majesty's cereal is kept in Tupperware.

I once stayed in a small hotel run by a former royal chef. Asked what the most difficult thing to cook for her Majesty was, he replied "The breakfast boiled egg. Her Majesty's only extravagance is the royal boiled egg. She likes them to be boiled to exactly the same consistency each morning. This is incredibly difficult, considering how old the egg is, what the hen feels like when it lays, etc. The only way to ensure consistency is to boil large quantities of different eggs.

Prince Charles, unfortunately, is the opposite in his tastes. A royal toothpaste squeezer on the one hand, and a frequent flyer on the other, which gives mixed messages about his supposed ecological tree-hugging credentials.

Assuming he eventually becomes the next King it would be interesting to see if he will be like Charles I (executed), or Charles II (spendthrift).

The main thing is that it doesn't matter too much anymore.

An Eccentric Building

No, I don't mean the buildings in Barcelona by Gaudi, fantastic as they are. I mean a hotel in London that I occasionally stayed at in the 1960s. The hotel was entirely dependent on the concierge. The switchboard was old-fashioned technology and depended on plugs being plugged in the right socket, with handles needing to be wound. Only the concierge understood it.

The lift was counterbalanced and operated by pulling a rope, with no electricity involved. Again, only the concierge understood how to stop exactly at the right floor.

Finally, there were no telephones in the rooms, but there was one telephone on each floor, located in the hall. When a call came in for a room, the concierge had to put a plug in the socket for the right floor, operate the rope lift to the floor, knock on the relevant door, and tell the occupant there was a call for him on the corridor phone. If he wasn't in, the concierge returned in the rope lift to his switchboard, and told the caller.

The concierge seemed to be aged about ninety, but was probably only forty, with the rest being the stress of the job.

Nowadays, it is a totally modernised and fashionable designer hotel. Paradoxically, it has a lot of problems with its lift, which must object to no longer being operated by rope.

An Eccentric Art Teacher

My art teacher had a magnificent beard. Sometimes, when he had washed his watercolour brushes, he would absentmindedly dry them on his beard. However, sometimes bits of colour remained on the brush after washing. He ended up with a beard of many colours. This also made it possible to work out how often he washed it.

Travel

The Royal View on Abroad

"I do not like abroad. I have been there," as stated by British King, George V.

The British View of Europe in the Early 1900s (Not Much has Changed Today)

Headline in the Times newspaper: "Fog in the English Channel, Europe Isolated"

The British Embassies Abroad—

Kazakhstan, Try to Get Us a Message from Prison in Office Hours

Kazakhstan twenty years ago was a very different place to what it is now, and a good example of how different abroad can be. The purpose of this anecdote is to reflect on British Embassies, not Kazakhstan.

The country is an authoritarian dictatorship. President Nazarbayev was the last Commissar of the Communist party upon the breakup of the Soviet empire.

After three unopposed elections, the international organisations declared, "No aid without elections." In the first election after that, unfortunately, the president's opponent was shot in a drive-by shooting two weeks before the election.

In the next election, Nazarbayev's son opposed him, but said all sensible people would vote for his father.

In order to get out of the country you have to have an exit visa, which then has to collect two dozen stamps on your boarding pass, right up to the steps of the aircraft.

My plane was leaving at 2.00 a.m. on a Sunday morning. My exit visa hadn't arrived by 10.30 p.m. on Saturday, so I phoned the British Embassy, foolishly thinking they would know what to do, since this could not be an isolated instance.

The embassy official I got through to said, "Unfortunately, I'm political. Consular is skiing this weekend and has said he is not to be disturbed. It seems you, therefore, do not have a plan B. I'll tell you what. If they do put you in prison, try to get a message to us in office hours."

You can compare this with the French and Dutch consular services, which have intelligence networks that work on an integrated basis with their large private sector companies. No wonder Britain slides down the tables of economic performance.

Best Travel Story

I was travelling from New Zealand to London, with one stop in the twenty-four hour flight in Los Angeles. The plane needed petrol and I needed a break. So, I had booked into the LAX Airport Hilton. This was one of those vast hotels with squillions of people milling about. Only the Americans and the Japanese can manage this type of hotel efficiently. I had never had any problems before, so I checked in and poured myself into bed. Next morning, greatly refreshed, I went down to breakfast.

The restaurant was total chaos. The head waitress must have been rehearsing for a movie, since she was inexplicably dressed like Peter Pan whilst pretending to fly through the dining room using her costume wings, and totally ignoring all that was happening with the customers. The waiters were Mexican and obviously untrained in the world of hospitality. They spoke no English at all, and I spoke no Spanish.

It looked like I would get no breakfast. Finally, I heard the voice of Wolfgang the German waiter. I called him over, and ordered in my very elementary German. Meanwhile, four air stewardesses sat at the next table. They looked round to see if anybody was listening, but were satisfied when I spoke German. I waved at them and said,

"Guten Morgen gnadige frauleins. Schlafen sie gut?" which translates into English as: "Good morning, gracious ladies. Did you sleep well?"

Well they certainly had. At that time there was an advertising slogan accompanied by a picture of a stewardess, which said "Fly me, fly United." I had not realised this was taken literally between the stewardesses and the pilots, but the stewardesses revelations were an eye opener.

The next time I stayed, I started with dinner. Hilton had solved the problem that none of their transient staff of waiters spoke a word of English. Each waiter had been taught one phrase and one action. I started with "a nice glass ice water", which was followed by "a nice glass of wine red white." I struggled with his total incomprehension of the wine list for a minute until I got the hang of the procedure. I also had "a nice hamburger", even though I didn't really want one.

The Scariest Flights

BEA Comet—The Emergency Door

My second ever flight, was in a BEA Comet. No, this is not a story about the wings giving way from metal fatigue; they found that out a few months later.

This was a flight to Rome from London. In those days nobody knew much about flying.

When we were in the air, about halfway to Rome, a small Italian boy who was totally unrestrained by his parents or the crew, ran to the emergency exit door, jumped on the seat next to it, and pulled the emergency exit handle. There was a hush, and then a sigh of relief when nothing happened. The loudest sound was the twenty or so Catholic priests on board all clicking their rosary beads at the same time.

Snow on the Pea Soup

The boy was too young to have grown up as Silvio Berlusconi.

(Her Majesty is reported to have said at a G8 summit in Britain when everybody was being held up for the group photo by Berlusconi, "Who is that very rude man holding us up by yelling into his mobile phone without stopping?")

Iberia Caravelle—Plane Buckets around the Sky

The Caravelle was a twin rear engine jet.

I was flying to Spain when the aircraft began bucketing round the sky. The crew panicked in Spanish only and wouldn't (or couldn't under stress) speak any English.

This problem of bucketing round the sky happened on other Caravelles, and so caused the aeroplane to be withdrawn soon afterwards.

Unpleasant Flights

Manx Airlines, The Reused Pork Pie

Manx Airlines, a subsidiary of British Midland, which happened to fly Mrs Thatcher on her campaigns, had a monopoly on the very lucrative flights to the Isle of Man from London. For those of you who do not know, the Island is a financial centre in the middle of the Irish Sea. British Midland, at the time, made these flights using twenty-five-year-old propeller Viscounts, a plane with few instruments.

On one flight, the captain put us down at Blackpool, on the west coast of England. He said he had circled the island twice, there was fog, he couldn't see the runway nor the equally important nearby Snaefell Mountain.

That was okay, but for companies holding a monopoly, the general attitude of not caring for the passengers (such as British Airways before privatisation) was unpleasant. Not to mention, the tickets were hugely expensive.

On one flight, I had an actuary with me to work on a pension fund on the island. He had never flown Manx before so I informed him ahead of time that the pork pie was foul and not to eat it.

He replied, somewhat confusingly, "With that, I must try it!" Being a mathematician, he cut an exact corner from the pie, took a bite, and after a moment's thoughtful chewing informed, "I agree. It's disgusting." I said, only in jest, "It's probably re-used from a previous flight."

On the way back, I was served the exact slice he had on our previous flight, with the precisely cut corner very evident!

American Airlines Express
(Commuter Airline to Small Cities)—Sludge in the Aisle

There was snow in the north eastern United States at Hartford, Connecticut. Twenty-five flights were waiting for pilots. Because of the snow, all the pilots in Hartford, or coming into Hartford, had used up their permitted hours. As can only happen in America, a plane eventually arrived from Florida full of pilots. The pilots joined their planes and the whole armada of was then able to take off.

My flight was on a Brazilian propeller plane, with a fearsome-looking stewardess who made it clear that she was there for the safety of the passengers and nothing else.

Eventually, someone called, "Miss, there's some sludge flowing down the aisle."

Her reply came in a very matter-of-fact way, "Don't make a fuss. It's only from the toilet, and it always happens on these airplanes." The way she said it made everybody too scared to say anything else.

Aerolineas Argentinios: Not All the Flights Made It Over the South Pole

Auckland, New Zealand to Buenos Aires via the South Pole was the route we were about to take with Aerolineas Argentinios. It was the rumour in New Zealand that some of their planes were believed to have disappeared, or made emergency landings at Argentine airbases. I followed advice to only take this route from New Zealand, as Qantas had set the computers in Sydney, and Air New Zealand subsequently checked them in Auckland.

Fortunately, the flight was fine with the only issue being, how did the stewardesses walk in the highest heels I have seen?

Singapore Airlines—Tight Skirts Around the Ankles = How Would They Be Able to Run in an Emergency?

On Singapore Airlines business class, drinks are served during the safety demonstration by stewardesses, who, as a lady colleague pointed out to me, were wearing national dress which involves skirts that are tight all the way down to the ankles. The meaning here is that they could only run in an emergency with difficulty.

Qantas, A Different Approach to Safety

A business class passenger was asleep during the safety demonstration aboard Qantas Airlines. He awoke to find a steward banging on the arm of his chair. He was told if he did it again he would become a banned passenger, and unable to fly Qantas again.

I once declared my shellfish allergy on Qantas. I couldn't understand why I was awakened by the steward to say, "Sorry, there was ham in your breakfast, so I'll remove it." This was done I thought to myself that this was odd since I hadn't said anything about ham. Then I noticed there was no chocolate.

I had worked it out. The airline computer programme had no way of computing a shellfish allergy, so the airline had taken me to the next major diet that did not allow shellfish, namely kosher!

Air New Zealand—A Total Failure at Controlling Very Drunk Passengers

In contrast, to the Qantas approach to safety, three spectacularly drunk passengers on the Tokyo to Auckland flight on board Air New Zealand, were allowed to not only board, but remain. Any competent airline would have denied them boarding. However, these three found it wildly amusing to keep yelling, "We're going to crash," which alarmed the Japanese person sitting next to me.

The disinterested stewardesses, rather than putting them in handcuffs, as would have been the procedure on any British airline, vacated the cabin and abandoned the other passengers.

Having recently seen BA crew quietly offloading a drunken passenger and taking a witness statement from a passenger, there are no excuses for being lax on safety.

Good Flights

Safety with Qantas

I was taking the world's longest flight from Sydney to Los Angeles across the Pacific. It involved fourteen solid hours without ever passing over land.

Just before take-off, the flight's female captain informed, "There is a flashing light on the console. Other airlines would either fly, using one of the two extra computer systems, or replace the light. On Qantas we fly safety by the book. I am ordering checks in case anything has failed. This will take three hours."

The total time on board was, therefore, extended to seventeen hours.

We had been scheduled to land before several scheduled Far East Airlines flights, which would have proved more time efficient due to the fact that almost every one of their passengers break American food quarantine laws. So when we arrived after having been delayed due to the necessary systems check, we were on the runway after Far East Airlines. This then caused another two hour delay. Nevertheless, every passenger was happy.

There are other airlines nearly as good, including British Airways, KLM, Swiss, and some American airlines.

Have a Drink on Us (Cyprus Airlines)

Early in my career, I was travelling in the economy class section whilst on holiday with my family. I noticed after quite some considerable time that the plane hadn't moved. Suddenly, there was a torrent of angry Greek words coming from the steward. I didn't know then that Greek, like Arabic, always sounds angry.

Then the steward switched to pure North London Greek-English, "Loidaies and Gennlemans, Coiprus Airloines is sorry for the deloi. It's not us; it's the air traffics, innit. So 'ave a drink on us."

The bars were rolled out and the passengers clapped.

Thanks that this Plane Flies Itself (British Airways in Kazakhstan)

Finally, I got on the pane to London from Alma Ata, Kazakhstan. At the time, this was a new service with British Airways., I collect the twenty-eight endorsing stamps needed on the exit visa (the last on the steps of the plane.)

It was an early Boeing 777. After a bit, I wondered where the crew were since I hadn't seen any since I had boarded. I went into the kitchen area and found one very miserable-looking stewardess.

I enquired as to the whereabouts of the other staff and she replied that they all had a violent stomach illness. Worriedly, I asked her if she had drunk the water and she told me that, yes, she had. She then showed me their written briefing, which specifically said the water was safe to drink.

"That's not quite right. This is one country where I brush my teeth with whisky and wrap a flannel round the tap so I do not drink tap water when confused in the middle of the night."

I had once passed a reservoir and there were two dead cows floating in it. There was a real problem with the breakup of the Soviet Union and only ethnic Russians were allowed to train as engineers, but they'd all gone.

I said at least ther are safety features in the airport to help take-off. "Surely the rotating radar at the airport helps?" I suggested.

She looked at her briefing notes and said, "What makes you think it's actually doing anything?"

She had a point. Thinking of the business class lounge at the airport with the springs sticking through the two sofas, and the map showing a building and indicated it to be the "Burn Terminal", I said that I understood.

Difficult Airports and Aeroplanes

Cook Islands

As we came in to land on the Cook Islands, I could see tiny bits of coral beneath the clear waters of the Pacific. I could also see that it had rained.

Fortunately, the Air New Zealand pilot was experienced. The strength of the braking necessary to land in such a small area was astounding. Once we were safely on the ground, the pilot informed all passengers, "Be glad I am Pacific island-experienced. Yesterday, an Air France pilot, fresh from Paris, didn't brake early enough and his 747 ended in the lagoon at Tahiti."

Snow and Ice

London's airports cease to be able to function with a few inches of snow on the ground. When the runways are finally cleared, there is a huge queue to spray de-icer on each plane using a hose attached to a tanker.

Imagine my surprise on one occasion when I flew via Reykjavik, as found that flying business class via Icelandair to Boston was cheaper than British Airways direct in world traveller class.

On this visit, the snow was tens of metres deep and the runways were kept clear by little Icelandic ladies who appeared totally circular, wearing several parkas each.

On leaving, the wind was blowing so hard that the big 767 planes were rocking at their gates. However, there was no delay on take-off, as the plane was de-iced by a carwash-like system, which only took a few seconds to spray the whole plane.

Concorde

A BA top level marketer told me the reason Concorde was so expensive was that the regular passengers that chose to take the flight on that iconic aircraft, had no idea what their tickets cost, and, furthermore, weren't bothered. They were the luxury jet set. I flew on it twice, both on BA's cheap deals at the end of its life.

The first inexpensive BA deal was called a Package Shakedown Cruise. We sailed from Istanbul to Venice, then flew Concorde from Venice to London.

How do you take a liner whose height was equal to eighteen stories above the waterline into Venice? Very carefully. During the cruise, the main problems were the toilets. They were malfunctioning in a big way and, strangely, would only flush in sequential order after dinner.

How do you fly out of Venice in the Concorde? As slowly as possible.

Fortunately for Venice, it didn't sink. The Concorde was not allowed to go supersonic until the Bay of Biscay.

The second BA deal I took advantage of was a specially priced standard trip from New York to London. This flight suffered a number of problems. The galley was out of the 1950s, so the food was poor. Secondly, they only had one case of wine. This was le Montrachet, the driest and one of the most expensive chardonnays. The first bottle was corked. Unfortunately though, mites had gotten into the cork, which had become porous. The wine had turned to pure vinegar, so a second bottle was opened. It was just the same. I found it inexcusable not to have an alternative wine.

Another problem was the passengers. I was seated next to an American investment banker with hair that was very dangerous because it stuck out to a great degree and was seemingly set with Ronseal. She had an attitude to match.

I noticed there was one spare seat on the plane and I attempted to contrive to either bag it myself, or influence my seatmate to take possession. Firstly, I tried a hacking cough. Unfortunately, that didn't work. I attempted a conversation in a fake northern accent about how cheaply I had bought the ticket. That didn't work either. Eventually, I tried scratching my head, pinching my fingers, and pretending to look between them. That worked. She fled to the free seat, and I was able to spread out.

Interesting Flights

Milan

I was waiting to take off with British Airways from Milan's Malpensa Airport during the Serbian War. Eventually the pilot announced, "I'm sorry air traffic control has said there will be a further thirty minute delay. We share air traffic control with a nearby Italian military airbase and there are eight Tornados and six F-14s ahead of us.

The Dutch View

During the Serbian War, I worked with a banker who was still in the reserves for the Dutch air force.

He asked me if I knew that the first Serbian MIG had been shot down by a Dutch pilot. The pilot had long hair which he wore in a hairnet, and his male gay partner, who was in the back, also had long hair.

He then added, "I don't understand all this military discipline in the UK. Hair length doesn't make any difference to the ability to press a button on a F-14."

Cars

The Number of Nieces in Monte Carlo

In Monte Carlo they routinely photograph your passport whenever you enter the Casinos' public rooms. They also do this when you enter the Casinos' private rooms, even though the general public does not have access.

I went in and discovered at the cheap tables for roulette, the chips were €700 each, and the more expensive tables, €7,000 Euros per chip. I fled.

However, in the evening, the real pleasure was standing outside the casino and seeing how the serious gamblers arrived. There was an average of ten Bentleys to each Ferrari, with no other make of car present at all. The Bentleys were chauffeur-driven for elderly gentlemen, and the few younger gamblers drove their own Ferraris.

You could easily discover who had won amongst the elderly gamblers. They came out with more teenage "nieces" on their arm than they had gone in with.

British Cars Before Mrs Thatcher

Britain had exchange control, which meant that buyers had to buy British. The British manufacturers took extreme advantage of their customers by selling them shoddy goods, as exchange control gave the buyers no choice.

Steam from Under the Bonnet

I bought a Reliant Scimitar. This was not the three-wheeler used by Del Boy in *Only Fools and Horses*. This was a snazzy sports car of the type favoured by Princess Anne. However, I soon found that it had a few minor faults.

The clutch moved the car forward even in neutral. To stop, I had to turn off the engine. The bodywork was made from plastic so that when you filled a scratch, the scratch continued spreading until major bodyworks were necessary to control the situation. These works would start with drilling holes all over to release the tension. The engine was the same as a speedy Ford Capri, but the radiator was mounted horizontally at the bottom, so it suffered badly from shocks whilst being driven on uneven roads. The cooling system was pressurised with hundreds of yards of coiled hosing, which kept on perishing due to steam inside the rubber cooling hose. There was also a lack of synchromesh in first gear and also a decided lack of power.

This was true, too, of the legendary Morris Minor. The estate car version had wood panelling. Very handsome and also very popular, but I knew one owner who carried a can of woodworm killer in the back.

I was brought up near North Wales with its mountains and sheep. The hills were not alive with the sound of music, they were full of the sound of unsynchronised gears of Morris Minors crunching during the double de-clutch procedure needed to get into first gear. Also, because the car was underpowered, farmers who had filled their cars with sheep, had to turn round and go up hills backward.

Even the first Morris Mini Minor was underpowered. In the age of flower power, minis would draw up at red lights on a dual carriageway next to US cars with huge engines and sporting large, sharp fins on the back. The minis would visibly vibrate as the young drivers prepared to speed off before the US cars. When the lights changed, the US cars would soundlessly take off and disappear into the distance with the aid of their five-litre engines. Note: The current mini was thereafter totally re-designed and re-engineered by BMW. It is still made in Oxford, where the originals first came off the assembly line.

Traffic Sign on Fiji

At about the time the old British traffic signs with words on them were being replaced by ones with pictures, on a roundabout in Fiji, where they drive on the left, there were two traffic signs together: An old-fashioned one saying, "Keep Left," and a new one saying, "Keep Right".

The Fake Maserati

My neighbour's Maserati is pale blue.

One morning I got up, said "Duh" as normal. Being half-awake and without my glasses, I opened the curtains.

Instead of seeing the usual blue car, there was a white one. I thought "Oh my God, the blue paint's washed off! They must have bought the Romanian fake."

It turned out it was a loan car, temporarily replacing my neighbour's which was being serviced.

Trains

Reasons for Running Late

A few years ago there were talkative drivers on the Thameslink train line.

"I'm sorry this train is late in arriving. That is because the train in front broke down."

"I'm sorry this train is late in arriving. That is because the train behind is late."

"I'm sorry this train is late in arriving. That is because it was late in departing."

"I'm sorry this train is late in arriving. That is because the train in front was late in arriving."

"I'm sorry this train is late in arriving. Like you, I haven't a clue as to why, because the signal box won't tell me."

I'm sorry we've stopped, but I've been told there is a dog loose in the tunnel. I'm an animal lover, and I've stopped the train to go and get him. When he announced he had the dog in his cab, everone clapped.

A passenger in a train crowded beyond belief shouted to the fool outside who was shouting for people to move along. "You can see how crowded the train is. What do you want us all to do mate, levitate?"

"Get off now at Cologne, we've coupled these sleeping cars to the wrong train . . .

. . . and if you stay on, you will end up in East Germany and be imprisoned."

This announcement was courtesy of West German Federal Railways, with the news they had coupled the sleepers for Vienna to a train going to East Germany (1963).

The Wrong Sort of Snow

In the late 1970s, the Bedford to London line was electrified and connected through some early twentieth century shallow tunnels under central London to the south. Because of the lack of height in the tunnels, the motor could not be accommodated in the usual position of under the overhead pantograph. They were, therefore, relocated under the railcars. This was fine for a few months until it snowed.

It was fine snow, which blew under the carriages and was then blown along by the cooling fans to hit the very hot engine, turning to water. In a week all eighty units were out of use for months.

Lovers Train, Netherlands

There was the brief privatisation of one line in the Netherlands and I travelled on it.

My pronunciation of the word *lovers* was corrected by a Dutch colleague to *loovers* because apparently, Mr Lovers is a person, and his name is pronounced "loovers>".

I responded with, "It is *lovers*, because I saw what happened on that train." The other main thing that went on was a party in the bar, complete with an accordion player and everybody singing and smoking cannabis.

The line was re-nationalised after voting by the rural MPs, because they claimed the masses of cannabis smoke coming out of the train windows was affecting the behaviour of the cows situated in the fields along the route.

The Dutch rural MPs are very powerful. They defeated a proposition to make English the official language of the Netherlands, because the cows wouldn't understand.

Trains and Rural Accounting

Many years ago, I was on a pay train, where the conductor collects the fares, as on a bus. It was in rural East Anglia. The ancient diesel was trying to outpace the fires on either side from burning wheat stubble.

We stopped at a station where a lot of people boarded. The guard looked at them and said in the local dialect, "Let's see. Four adult, five childer, three pushchair, and four dawgs. Wait minute. Wait minute. Oi can't add that up. Gi'us twenty pound. It's orl wrang, but it'll be orl roight."

This is illustrative of the typically unique thinking in the area. Only recently, I was told a seaside café was closed. When I queried the owner as to when his closing time was, he replied, "In ten minutes."

Similarly, an elderly member of the local Women's Institute, who was in charge of the local accounts, happened to be compiling them whilst a meeting was going on. At the end of the meeting she informed the group, "I am very pleased to say we have a surplus of £900 and I have no idea why. Then she looked again at her handwriting and corrected, "Oh, sorry, it's not £900, but nine pounds no pence."

Horses with Night-time Lighting

In these difficult times for police budgets, cuts have abolished many mounted police. In the Norfolk Broads, the safest part of the country, horses were abolished. The PCs were then allowed to become mounted police again, but only if they provided their own horse.

The City of London has money coming out of its ears, which is good considering the amount of GDP that comes from there. As has been tradition, other police forces have ordinary riding horses, which are trained to work in riots. The City police have carthorses, or shires. They are trained to walk sideways, and thus push rioters in one direction.

One day at about 5.00 p.m. at the start of the rush hour, I was standing outside Liverpool Street Station in the City. The traffic in the next street, Bishopsgate, was already solid, with drivers using their horns with impatience. Two of the huge City police horses came into sight, ridden by small WPCs.

They were lit, with a white light attached to their manes in front, and a red light attached to their tails. The two horses were made to walk very slowly to the corner of Bishopsgate. Their riders then spent fifteen minutes practicing parade ground drill, getting the inner horse to go round the corner marking time and the outer horse to ride a bit faster, so that it was exactly the same length away from the inner horse.

The motorists in the Bishopsgate queue wisely kept their cool, up to the first bus. Behind that, they could not see the police horses, and were getting livid at the delay, until the mounted police called for assistance.

Of This and That

Tea in Harrods with Secret Agents?

One day I decided to try tea in Harrods for the first time. Just tea, which I consider to be the best way to try the standards of English breakfast tea.

When the tea was served, I poured, obviously aiming for the cup. Suddenly, I found the table was flooded. The teapot looked as if someone had sawed off the spout! I wondered why should this be and my imagination took over.

In the end, I concluded it must be about the endless dispute between Argentina and Britain over the Falklands. This was a new Argentinian tactic. Teams of smartly dressed Argentinian commandos were being sent to have tea at Harrods to damage the teapots.

In my imagination, one operative would cleverly hold up a napkin to prevent the noxious crime from being observed, whilst the other commando would saw off the spout of the teapot. When all the teapots had been sabotaged, there would be no chance of drinking tea in Harrods again. Britain would then surrender the Falklands, provided Argentina gave the teapot spouts back.

The English Tea Habit

The majority of British people pour milk into their cup before the tea. The majority of European people do the opposite. Does it matter? I believe it does. It certainly mattered for an English spy in Germany in the early days of the war. He poured milk into his tea first. His hosts had never seen this before, and reported him to the Gestapo.

Filet Americaine

Many Americans make the mistake of ordering this in Belgium and are shocked when it arrives. They expect a T-bone steak. In reality, filet Americaine is an alternative name for steak tartare, which is raw minced steak, mixed with raw egg yolk, finely chopped shallots, and capers.

As my Belgian colleague said, "I only eat this in restaurants where I know the uneaten portions are thrown away at the end of the day."

Interestingly, in connection with the recent scandal of supermarkets serving horsemeat labelled as beef, in France, Steak Tartare is normally made with horsemeat, as there is less chance of it developing unpleasant infectious bacillae.

Is There a German Sense of Humour?

German people do have a sense of humour, of course, but it's very different from that of other Europeans.

At the very northern end of the North Island of New Zealand, there is a ninety mile beach of golden sand. Entry onto the beach is forbidden to cars and this is evident by the posting of multiple notices. These notices warn of quick sands and rip tides that can occur with little or no warning. Everyone is told to use only the four-wheel drive buses available for hire, which are piloted by specially trained drivers who do not travel when the beach is dangerous

The previous week, the drivers of a Honda had ignored the warnings, and had been caught by a rip tide. The vehicle flipped over, and the people within had to be airlifted to hospital.

Three days later, I was one person in a group that consisted of a few German people who took the four-wheel drive bus along the sands. Whilst on our visit, we stopped to have a look at the overturned Honda. Within three days, the Honda was 90 per cent submerged in the sand. When we got out for a closer look, all the Germans started laughing. I asked them what they were laughing at and was told it was very funny. I asked them what was funny, and they said what they felt was amusing was the fact that the Honda was submerged and the Mercedes four-wheel drive bus just continued normally.

It may not be our sense of humour, but it is a sense of humour.

Most Useful Advice from an MP

I once worked for a firm of stockbrokers in Birmingham whose senior partner was Anthony Beaumont Dark. Tony, as he preferred to be called, had been an elected politician since before he was able to vote. When I knew him, he was the elected finance director of West Midlands council. This was in the early days of computing, and we were not allowed to refer to the time when he defeated his own budget by pressing the wrong button on his computer.

He managed to be the amazing bridge between the two sides of society in the 1970s. He was an unashamed Conservative, driving to his stockbroking job in his Rolls Royce. However, he was also elected as MP for Selly Oak, the British Leyland constituency at a time of extreme militancy. He had a mini to drive in that constituency. He did this because he said and believed in the British working man.

A lot of bitterness would have been avoided in the whole country if Mrs Thatcher had listened to him. Instead, she hated him and put her acolytes onto hounding him. Once, she passed him in the Commons lobby, and said, sarcastically, "Voting with us today, Beaumont?" It is believed this stress and its side effects helped cause his early death.

Anyway, to close on a happier note, before I left his firm, he said he had some advice based on his years in politics. "Chris, If you see the s*   *   * about to hit the fan, duck." Pity he was too honest to do that himself.

Y vonnae vae veg (Manx Gaelic)

The Isle of Man sits in the Irish Sea between England and Ireland. On the main road between the airport and Douglas, there is a bridge labelled "Fairy Bridge." Fairy is their word for spirit, or troll. When local people cross the bridge in their cars, they touch their foreheads and mutter something. On enquiring, I found it was "Y vonnae vae veg", which is a surviving part of the almost-lost Manx Gaelic. It means pay respect to the fairies (little people).

There apparently used to be monastery at the bridge before the reformation. When the monastery was there, people passing had to tip their hats in respect to the monks. Over time, they forgot why they were tipping their hats, so the legend grew that it was because little people lived there. Hence, in addition to tipping their hats, they said hello to the little people.

There was actually some justification. In the 1930s a bus of schoolgirls passed over the bridge, and they yelled insults at the little people. The back window of the bus blew out. This helped the power of the legend.

France—Vive La Difference

London Hotels in the Old Days, Cereals, and the French

Believe it or not, we have forged a closer relationship with the French in recent years. In the 1970s, I was staying in what passed for a hotel in a smart part of London. There was an eccentric scene at breakfast. At that time, breakfast cereals did not exist in France. The Frenchman at the next table had obviously not seen cornflakes before. He was eating them dry with a fork, with noises that indicted eating them in that way was painful.

Wellington Won the Battle but Napoleon Won the War

In truth, our problems with the French are not based on Napoleon as a soldier, but Napoleon as a bureaucrat. Napoleon's influence is still paramount in France, and most of Europe, which is why the English don't understand Europe.

Wellington won the battle of Waterloo, but Napoleon won the war. The administrative system introduced into France after the Revolution by the French is still in place today, and is the basis of the way the European Union operates. As an example of its centralised control from Paris (which explains how rude Parisians are, because they consider they come from the centre of the universe and everyone else is inferior), the French minister of education can say what any school in France is teaching at any time of day, on any day in the year.

In contrast, British logic is bottom up: If I do this and it goes bang in the same way several times, then it must be true. French logic is top down: so if the state says it will not go bang, then the readings must be wrong.

If only the UK would adopt the French code of justice, we would have no problems with human rights. France has nearly 100 per cent nuclear power because when people protested when the nuclear power stations were being built, the CRS (Compagnies Républicaines de Sécurité or, riot police) hit them over the head until they went away.

The French Interpretation of the EU Human Rights Law:

Get the Fire Brigade to Flush Them Out

I recently stayed at a wonderful monastery that had been converted into a luxury hotel. The testimonials in the lobby from de Gaulle and Eisenhower to the owners and the local butchers, described them as genuine heroes of the resistance. This made them legends in the area.

The owners also had a derelict building nearby, which they were trying to turn into another hotel. It had been squatted in by peaceful painters and artists. When the hotel wanted possession, the police and SAMU (the fire brigade) arrived. First SAMU took out their big axes and removed the windows. Then they flushed the squatters out with hoses. The CRS (riot squad) hit the artists on the head as they left the building, to help persuade them not to do it again.

We in the UK despair of getting enough clean renewable energy. Perhaps consider that France is 100 per cent nuclear. This came about after the early demonstrations against nuclear power were dealt with in the same way by the CRS.

So much for human rights in the EU. Do not blame Europe for Abu Qatada's human rights, blame British governments, in particular, lawyers, for their interpretation of the human rights law which maximises lawyers' fees and minimises justice. Roll on the day when we realise this and appoint a Frenchman as Justice Secretary!

French Unpasteurised Food

Even the food the French people eat is different from what an English person would expect. In England, the doctors are always warning against unpasteurised food. The French medical view is totally different. Their view is that frequent exposure to unpasteurised food from a young age gives immunity when you are older because the bugs in unpasteurised food can be dangerous. (Note: I am not medically qualified, so ask your doctor.)

At a French Saturday market in a small town, the longest queue was at an unattended table. Eventually, a French peasant farmer appeared with one churn. Apparently, it contained the milk of his only cow, still warm and totally untreated. The folks in the queue all produced their own containers, varying from open jugs to old coca cola bottles. They were all duly filled with the warm milk, and five minutes later the stall was deserted again.

In another example of how the French believe exactly the opposite to the English, they espouse that maximum antibiotics are good for you. A colleague became ill with influenza while at a conference in Monte Carlo. A local Monacan doctor prescribed three antibiotics. My colleague was cured in two days, as opposed to the British view that influenza is a virus, so antibiotics would therefore be useless. A good many of the medical professors who write about antibiotics being bad for you end up with knighthoods. Is this just a happy accident, or could it be because expounding that point of view happens to have the knock-on effect of saving the National Health Service millions? I would be curious to know what happens to the professors who point out why the French, practicing the exact opposite, live so much longer.

I had a similar instance, with flu on a flight to Australia. As there is no doctor at Heathrow (a criminal omission), I went to a doctor when I stopped over in Singapore. He said to me, "We are at the crossroads of the world. Take this western antibiotic, these Japanese nose drops, and this Chinese medicine. Do not ask what is in the Chinese medicine." I was better the next day.

Luxembourg and France with Banking Secrecy

"With this, Luxembourg has to go back to milking the coos."

The French peoples' view of Britain is that we are incredibly ignorant of Europe, and thus easily manipulated, which happens to be rue.

There was a cross-country, cross-professional meeting at the bank when a 10 per cent withholding tax on dividends throughout Europe was proposed.

At the time, both Luxembourg and Austria had bank accounts whose ownership was difficult to trace. Those in Luxembourg wishing not to pay their national taxes hold bearer bonds, being fixed interest certificates, which are not registered to an individual in their banks. On dividend day, you can find a queue of expensive chauffeur-driven Mercedes each sporting one passenger in an expensive suit. The passengers each get out with a briefcase, enter the bank, and return to the vehicle with a much heavier briefcase. The queue stretches from Luxembourg City to the German border.

The issue of raising this tax is now finally being settled with a typically European compromise. But, at the time that was not clear.

The first to address those gathered for the meeting were two French-speaking lawyers from Luxembourg called Jacques and Jules. Their English was delightful. Jules made his feelings known when he stated, "Jacques, this new law will be terrible for Luxembourg. With this, we will have to go back to milking the coos."

Jacques replied with, "Do not worry, there is no problem."

"There cannot be no problem. This means le wipe-out for Luxembourg and Austria for concealing money from the Eastern European authorities. Luxembourg uses the veto for the first time? That is not at all communitaire. That is shame for Luxembourg," was Jules' reply.

Jacques stated, "No problem. Angleterre (England) will use the veto."

Jules again replied, "Why? This is potential wipe out for Luxembourg and Austria, but there is no problem for Angleterre."

Jacques clarified, "Exactly. But les Anglais are ignorant and stupid, and they don't know that."

Sure enough, a couple of weeks later, England used the veto to save a handful of jobs, and the Luxembourgers and Austrians, whose countries were facing job losses in the tens of thousands, laughed at us.

Why Do the French Live Much Longer Than Us?

The last laugh is to the French. They live 5 per cent longer than we do, which is statistically enormous. Their healthcare is diametrically opposed to ours. They drink lots of wine, whose health benefits have finally been accepted by the Puritan-dominated British medical establishment through their gritted teeth. There is even a pill made from an extract of grape skin, which protects against heart disease. This is a boon for religious teetotallers and is much-consumed in the Southern United States.

Medical ethics were much simpler long ago. There was only the oath of Hypocrites to take, which originated from ancient Greek times. Interestingly, I have read that 98 per cent of US doctors still take this oath, but only 50 per cent of English doctors. What frightens the English doctors about the Hippocratic Oath? Is it the knowledge of the less-than-ideal treatments sometimes dictated by NHS management on cost grounds?

French Views in Other Areas that are Radically Different from Britain's

I present an anecdote to show how fundamentally different the French are from the British:

I visited a big French company when I was working with an oil reserve fund. I sat next to the Managing Director at lunch. I had an opportunity to speak to him, and so I asked, "I note that you are bidding for the French telephone manufacturing company. How does this really work?"

He replied in his heavy French accent, "Ze gouvernement telephones us. They say, we 'ave zees company, Locatel. It makes ze telephones, but does not 'ave ze good marketing. You 'ave ze marketing. So you bid for zem, then we 'ave ze compagnie la France can be proud of.

"We say mais non. We 'ave ze marketing, zey 'ave ze manufacturing, but you are ze gouvernement. You 'ave ze monnaie. First you give us ze monnaie, zen we buy zees compagnie. Then we 'ave ze compagnie la France can be proud of."

It worked. France was transformed from a country with some of the worst telephones in Europe to one of the best.

How could the French government know so much detail about individual companies? In Britain, civil servants pride themselves on their ignorance of worldly things. In France, it is the opposite.

The French universities have no entrance exam, thus the early years lectures are grossly overcrowded. The ruling class go instead to small technical institutions, the Ecole Normales, instituted by Napoleon. The senior of them is the Ecole Normale Superior. Its members move, during their careers, between the Civil Service, Industry, and Politics. At any stage, they can ask; informally, for the knowledge of an issue of any former member of their Ecole.

French Food and a Bit of History, Too

I personally give the cooking prize to France. This is not for a traditional dish taking hours to cook and costing an arm and a leg at a ludicrously over-the-top restaurant. This is for a dish I enjoyed at a simple French café in the Pas de Calais.

The plastic menu in the café simply said "le Welch." I worked this out as Welsh Rarebit. Not to be confused with Welsh Rabbit, i.e., cheese on toast served to the Methodist, therefore teetotal, Welsh people. This was proper Welsh rarebit: toast with melted cheese, beer, and mustard.

This is served on a slice of bread which is then baked to make the liquid mixture set. The French version had French bread at the bottom of a soup plate, which had been filled with the runny mixture. This French adaptation of a traditional British dish was impressive.

The café was in Agincourt (known in French as Azincourt), and I was in good humour after visiting the museum dedicated to the famous battle. The script of the film the visitor centre showed finished with "The dastardly English fired their arrows from hiding. Nowadays the village . . ."

There was nothing about the brilliant choice of battlefield by Henry V. The French charged into a funnel. There was a wood in the bottom right of the field, and the bottom left was obstructed by a triangle of English stakes (every English archer carried two big sharpened stakes.). The legendary English archers were concealed in the wood.

As the French knights charged, they got stuck in the funnel between the wood and the stakes. Then the English archers fired into the air above the French so the speed of the arrows penetrated the horses' armour.

The sheer weight of the French knights' armour meant when they fell with their horse, they stayed down.

After a Lot of Banging, the Hot Water Tap in the Bath Eventually Disgorged a Puddle of Brown Water

The most interesting place I visited in France was probably Turckheim. It is a tiny village in Alsace in French wine making country. Alsace is between Strasbourg and Basel in east of France. The Eastern border is the River Rhine. This wide stretch of water provides a microclimate for the vines, which are planted on the facing slopes of the hills nearby.

Turckheim is a really old village. The warden goes round the walls at curfew time, singing in old Alsatian in a language that, interestingly, is a variety of mediaeval German.

Our hotel had been stayed in by Napoleon and Charles de Gaulle, and not modernised since. A lot of fiddling with the taps in the bath eventually produced a banging sound and a small amount of brown water.

However, the various pastries available for breakfast were astounding, as were the vineyards. There was a contrast with the modern as our route into the village was initially blocked by the Tour de France. The next day, Lance Armstrong was in the lead in the mountain stage. The French government, or someone, had bribed the nearby Unilever workers to jump out of the forest in front of Lance and make him fall off his bike. However, given the drugs he was on, he probably wasn't bothered.

At that time we rented a row of vines (in actuality, we were able to buy some cases from a winemaker who hated negotiants (middlemen); so instead, they sold it directly to registered customers. He took us round his vines and explained that no land had changed hands in Alsace winemaking in over a decade. It is strictly a father-to-son business. Uniquely, several varieties of grapes are grown together. There would be a row of pinot fris, two rows of gewürztraminer, four rows of riesling, etc. To the casual observer, these appear to be laid out at random.

I asked the winemaker how he knew which variety to plant where. He told me, "I plant the same way as done by my great, great, great, grandfazzer. He knew."

This shows the importance of tradition in France.

French Juniper Gin

This normally comes from the Netherlands, where it is known as Jenver. However we found a tiny distillery in the north east of France. We were told, with pride, that the distilling machinery had been in place since 1850, and nothing had changed in the manufacturing process since then. The owner had been given one of the rarest French decorations—the Legion d'Honneur Agricole (agricultural.)

We passed through the bottling room. There were the open bottles of gin. There was an ancient peasant in a beret putting on the labels and putting in the corks very slowly. He was smoking a cigarette that bore an amazing amount of ash at the end. Suddenly, all the ash fell into an open bottle. The peasant carried on, not noticing, and put in the cork.

Health and safety in France would not dare inspect the premises of someone with the Legion d'Honneur Agricole.

Actuaries and Accountants—
Mathematical Geniuses at Work

Actuaries are one of the least-known professions. I spent many years working with them. Think of first class honours in maths, and only about a quarter qualifying at the end of seven years. They work basically on building mathematical models of average life expectancy for a group of people in a pension scheme. For example, the statistics show that ex-coal miners will live less long than a group of lawyers.

As a result of being mathematicians and working on the gloomy job of predicting average years of death, their reputation is of being pretty introverted. This has some truth in it, although there are plenty who are extroverted.

Their reputation leads to a number of jokes. For example:

"How can you tell an extroverted actuary? In the underground train, he looks at your shoes, not his own."

"How many actuaries does it take to change a light bulb? 1,000. One to go up a ladder, then give up when he reads the results of the mathematical model from the other 999 which proves it cannot be done because they forgot to factor in that the light bulb can turn"

The Actuary and the Model

The only joke my colleagues found funny was:

"A young actuary goes into a bar. He finds he is sitting next to a very attractive young lady.

She says to him, "What do you do?"

He replies, "I'm an actuary. What do you do?"

She replies, "I'm a model."

He says, "Funny, you don't look like one!" (Crib: he was thinking of a mathematical model.)

The Actuaries and the Cannabis-Coloured Sweets from the Netherlands

My best joke played on the actuaries occurred when I joined my last employer after working with the Dutch. I did contribute a bag of Hopjes, which are the Dutch's' favourite wrapped sweets. They are brown in colour.

One of the actuaries said, "These are very nice, Chris. What are they made of?"

I replied, "Well, they are the Dutch's favourite. I'm not exactly sure, but as they are brown and the Dutch like them, so it's probably Cannabis."

There was an immediate noise of spitting into bins. (Actually, they're flavoured with coffee.)

Cambridge—An Oxford Joke

I don't know much about it other than it's a relatively new university compared to Oxford, and in a very cold part of the country. They also punt with poles, but from the wrong (flat) part of the punt. I don't know how they do this without falling into the water.

In my day, colleges locked their gates at twelve midnight. A couple of Oxford undergraduates had found their college scarf was exactly the same as that worn at a Cambridge College. They went to Cambridge and waited until after midnight. When they saw a couple of proctors (university police attired in suits and bowler hats), they started running. The proctors ran after them. Eventually they let the proctors catch them.

The proctors said, "Which college of the university do you belong to, sirs? We recognise the scarves you are wearing."

The two Oxford undergraduates replied, "University? University? We didn't know there was a University here. Was it built recently? Because our university is the oldest in Britain, and is located along the Thames."

Eventually, just before I retired, we went to Boston, USA. I was able to send a postcard to our chief actuary (operational) who went to Cambridge. The card read, "At last I have found Cambridge." Harvard was pictured on the front of the postcard over the picture of Harvard Yard. Harvard is in Cambridge County, Massachusetts.

I got on well with most of the actuaries because of complementary skills.

One day, the senior partner of my first firm called me to one side and said he had been most interested to discovered that I read history as a subject, since everyone else was a boring first class honours in maths.

He didn't know about the one who read geography. I asked the geographer why, he had become an Actuary since the exams must have been even worse for him than for others reading maths. He said, "I couldn't get a job."

Actuarial Communication Skills

I was sympathetic to the nervous, high-powered actuary in my first firm. He was so upset when he couldn't get the new Asset Liability Model to work, and the other actuaries kept calling him thick, so that he could only eat bananas. I was nice to him, and he explained what the model did in very simple terms to me, which was just what I needed.

The Best Actuarial Talk

Unlike most of the actuaries where I worked, I was strong at communicating. The best communication I saw from an actuary was by accident. In a life company, where I was Investment Manager, my colleague who managed International Equities, had lines of letters after his name.

On this occasion, he had to speak about our new Japan fund. Since this was the first unit-linked Japan fund, nobody knew much about the subject. His audience were stockbrokers, so there was a potential for disaster because there was a high chance they wouldn't understand anything he said. I certainly thought that might be the case after reading his draft speech.

He was incredibly nervous, and after the first couple of words, knocked his papers, which he had failed to staple together, onto the floor. He got more and more flustered, because he couldn't find the first page of his speech. Eventually, he said to the waiting audience, "Sorry, I can't find my speech. All I can say is it's a fine fund, and I suggest you stuff your clients' money into it."

It brought the house down, and the fund brought in incredible amounts of money. In his panic, he had accidentally hit all the right buttons. Here was a message they could understand about a very difficult subject, from an incredibly intelligent person.

Once a younger actuary asked for my advice on possible venues when his then-girlfriend, also an actuary, said she wanted to attend a nice dinner and hear a classical music concert. I thought about it a while and suggested a concert of nice classical music at the Festival Hall and a dinner at their very good restaurant which included a table overlooking the river. In turn, he volunteered to do three asset liability studies for me.

The basic business of actuaries is final salary pension funds. These occur where the company assumes the liability of paying an income in retirement to its members. The company must, therefore, try to match that income long in advance by assets. Final salary pension funds are in very slow decline. The life of the pension fund can be many decades after it closes to new members. It lasts until the last member dies. If an eighty-year-old marries, say, one of the Cheeky Girls aged thirty, the Cheeky wife will get a widow's pension, until she dies.

But Actuaries are Very Different in Brazil

Brazilian Lady Actuaries

In other countries, actuaries are different because the culture is different.

At the end of my first visit to Brazil, which lasted a week, I was asked if there was anything more I needed. I said I wished to gain more technical knowledge and asked to see a couple more Brazilian actuaries.

At the appointed time, a couple of attractive girls arrived, looking like Cariocas (girls from the beaches in Rio). Thinking about what they looked like, I thought they must be from the marketing department.

Slightly sarcastically, I enquired, "So, which of you is the actuary?"

To my surprise, they responded, "Both of us."

"So how many actuaries are there in Brazil?"

One lady replied, "Five hundred," but at the same time, the other said, "Two thousand."

The second one asked her colleague, "How can there only be five hundred? My registration number is 1250?"

The first replied, "Because this is Brazil. A lot have probably died without telling us."

Making Lots of Money as an Actuary

On another occasion, I was visiting an elderly male actuary. His firm had sent a young American actuary to find out how his practice, which operated from his own office in Sao Paolo, made so much money.

"How long does it take to qualify in Brazil?" I asked.

Looking at the young American actuary, he replied in a strong Brazilian accent, "It would take this young American actuary many, many years. Have to pass examen in mathematic, economic, Brazile history and geographe. Brazile history and geographe ver ver complicate."

Accountancy Jokes

I don't know much about accountants. The ones I know have varying personalities. When you get to the top of the profession, such as a partner at Ernst & Young, you have people of broad understanding who work incredibly long hours. Anyway, here are two jokes.

Prague Zoo, Czech Republic

One of the lions at Prague Zoo in the Czech Republic escapes, and eats a keeper. Nobody sees it. Both the lions were caught, and the staff were trying to decide which lion to shoot. They all decided the female looked guilty. They were about to shoot it, when the zoo's finance director, an accountant, arrives and asks what is going on.

They tell him and he quickly says, "Stop. You're wrong."

"How do you know," they ask.

He says, "Because the cheque's/check's always in the male."

I told my firm's finance director that joke, and he said "Very good. But what's the point?"

Of course the point of a joke is that it has no point.

The French Hot Air Balloonist

The second joke involves a hot air balloonist.

He takes off in northern France. Strong winds from the south take him over the Channel, and he comes down somewhere in Kent with no idea exactly where he is.

He sees some commuters walking down the lane to the station smartly dressed in suits with umbrellas and bowler hats. He shouts out, "Hello, can you please tell me where I am?"

One of the commuters shouts back, "You are standing in a gondola under a balloon, in the middle of a field."

The balloonist replies "Ah. You must be an accountant."

"Good heavens," replies the accountant, "how did you know?"

"Because," said the balloonist, "your information is totally correct. It is also totally useless."

Most of the jokes are in the vein of the definition of bankers: people who will lend you an umbrella when it's not raining.

Australian Airport Humour

On my first visit to Sydney on board British Airways, we had to fly around Sydney for over an hour. The pilot had told us it was because we were early and we had to conform to Sydney's noise control regulations banning early landings.

The arrivals hall was empty when we eventually landed. I was one of the first at Immigration. The customs officer yelled, "The Poms are here at last."

He said to me, "Where have you all been?"

I replied that we were late due to air traffic control informing the BA pilot that the airport was closed till 8.00 a.m.

He yelled, "Got another rookie Pommie pilot!"

He then told me that there are no noise restrictions, but they always try it on with the Pommie pilots the first time they land in Sydney.

Upon leaving the customs hall, the condom machine in the men's lavatory had graffiti written on it which stated, "In the event of complaint, post baby in slot."

A Less Pleasant Arrival in Australia

Tony Wedgwood Benn, who was an ultra-left Minister in the 1970s ("All my life I have dreamed of nationalising everything."), was being examined by a very unpleasant customs official upon entering Australia.

The customs official held up Mr Benn's passport and said, "Any criminal convictions?" Tony said "I didn't know they were still required."

(Thanks to my doctor for that one.)

Ayers Rock from the Air

The second time I visited, I travelled on Qantas and we were treated to a great view of Ayers Rock. Ayers Rock, or Uluru, towers above the scrub desert of the "red centre" of Australia. It is one of the few features of the earth visible from 30,000 feet. Other great sights include the Grand Canyon, the Mekong in flood, and the French ex-colonial red roofs of Vientiane.

The pilot announced, "Ladies and gentleman, boys and girls, I gather those of you on the right of the plane have had a great view of Ayers Rock, but those on the left haven't seen it. So, I will just circle around so those on the left can see it.

You can imagine air traffic control at Alice Springs, where a controller stops whatever he's doing, and says, "Fine, Mate," to the pilot of a huge aircraft, which then makes a 380 degree turn covering hundreds of miles.

What panic would there be if anyone tried that at Heathrow, with thousands of planes having to be diverted.

Ayers Rock from the Ground

In fact, Ayers Rock is one of the most difficult places in the world to get to, with flights being booked months in advance. That is because, apart from a day or so every few decades when it rains and the red centre comes alive with long dormant flowers, there is no rain or any underground aquifers. Everyone wants to see sunset and sunrise at Ayers Rock, and to do this, they all need a hotel for the night. Because of the shortage of water, however, there are very few hotels. So where does their water come from? It has to come by water tanker train from Adelaide. The distances are so huge that it takes a week for this train to make the journey.

During a much later visit, I managed to get to Ayers Rock and see the sunset. The guide said it was astonishing that about one in two ladies who climbed the Rock did so in high heels, despite being told to remove them. A high proportion ended with broken ankles.

Japanese Tourists at the Sydney Opera House

The front two rows of the Sydney Opera House always seemed to be occupied by Japanese tourists. During one performance, about three quarters of the way through the first act, the front two rows of Japanese tourists stood up and filed out. Another two rows' worth of Japanese people filed in and took their places. Naturally, there was an enquiry because of the disruption to both audience and cast.

It turned out that the tourists were on organised tours. Before the programme began, there was an announcement that the performance would begin three quarters of an hour late as the principal tenor had a sore throat. The Japanese tour guide didn't understand a word. In Japan everything runs precisely to time. She also knew nothing about opera. When her watch got to the time her itinerary said her party should leave, she told them to leave. The reason was that there were two groups of Japanese visiting the opera. Both had been sold a half-performance and a half-harbour cruise for over £1,000. The actual retail cost of this package was under £100 each, representing a huge profit margin for the Japanese tour agents.

Other Countries

Panic in the Grand Canyon

In the early 1980s, we took a small plane from Phoenix to see the Grand Canyon. We actually flew inside the Grand Canyon.

Out of nowhere, there was a violent electrical storm. The plane was being buffeted around, and was hit by lightning. The pilot was a model of Southern calm. He was reassuring us over the radio and telling us there was no problem, whilst drinking coke and smoking a cigar at the same time. We eventually landed.

However, despite the calm of the pilot, the rules of flying in the Grand Canyon have since changed and planes are now forbidden from entering the Canyon itself. It seems other flights after us were not so lucky in storms, and several were blown into the sides of the canyon.

How Come Brazilian Airlines Can Serve a Full Breakfast in the Time it Takes BA to Serve a Bacon Roll?

My first flight from Sao Paolo to Brasilia on board Rio Sul, a domestic Brazilian airline, had me wondering. Why was it that during a flight of approximately the same length as a flight from London to Manchester, a Brazilian airline is able to serve a full breakfast in the same amount of time that it takes BA to serve a bacon roll?

After observation, I was able to solve this conundrum. Five Brazilian stewardesses are so thin, that they can pass at the same point in the aisle at the same time.

The tiny cups of coffee on Brazilian flights are optional. Each cup contains the equivalent of an entire coffee plantation. Italian ristretto, eat your heart out.

Mechanical Problems

Replacement Plane

BA Edinburgh—London. The British Airways plane was cancelled for mechanical problems. A charter plane replaced it, and we boarded The Captain announced "I'm sorry, we seem to have a problem. Fortunately, I know how to fix it, as it's happened before. Fortunately this airline carries a full set of spares." The Pilot walked through the cabin waving a screwdriver. Everyone cheered.

Islands in the Sun

At this stage, I am reminded of a spoof Pathé pictorial travelogue which was done in the same format as the short films they used to present in cinemas before the main film.

It starred Peter Sellers, and was called "Balham, Gateway to the Sun". It featured a fictional toothbrush manufacturing factory in

Balham, South London. Peter Sellers played the factory worker being interviewed.

A portion of the interview went thusly, "I work in the toothbrush factory putting in the bristles. It is skilled work, so it has to be done manually, which is to say, once a year."

Isle of Man

I had clients in the Isle of Man, which has to be admired not the least for making a profit from the sale of postage stamps.

Continuing on in the airline theme, Manx Airlines' BAe146 small short take off and landing jet, as used in the USA from Denver to Aspen was out of action. This happened frequently after rain due to the fact that there was a big dip in the runway, and passing through the dip caused the standing water to be sucked into the four engines.

At the same time, the Viscounts were being serviced, so a Boeing 737 was chartered. The cockpit door was open and as the plane screeched to a stop about ten yards from King William's Chapel, the pilot was heard to exclaim, "My God! That's the nearest I have got to totalling a plane!"

In another incident on the Isle of Man, I was invited to a dinner being held in a restaurant. I was not feeling hungry, so, having had duck the night before in a London restaurant, which was three or four tiny slices, I thought I would order it again. There was almost no conversation, because the islanders knew everything about each other. The only conversation between my two nearest seating companions came after a quarter of an hour and consisted of one saying hello to the other and nothing more.

Eventually, my dinner arrived. It is easy to forget that, in addition to holidays and financial services, this is a farming country, situated about the same latitude as the North of England. My duck dish arrived, and it was a whole roast duck. To make it gourmet, the chef had removed the feet. When I stuck my fork in, it became dislodged from the plate, and my dinner rolled all the way down our table of thirty people.

Once, when we got to our hotel, we were given our room keys for Rooms 230 and 231. When we got to the corridor, the numbers went up from 200 to 229, and then down to 200 again, so there were two rooms each with numbers to 229, but our rooms did not exist. We went back to reception to enquire about this and the receptionist said they were in the middle of renumbering the rooms, which didn't really help us at all.

At least this was better than at another hotel, now closed, where the waitress thought boiled eggs for breakfast were scary, so they took an hour.

The Cook Islands

Slow breakfasts are my link from the Isle of Man to the Cook Islands, which appear as the classic tiny dots in the middle of the Pacific. These islands are inhabited by the Maori people and are run with a self-governing democracy where external affairs are handled by New Zealand.

The combination of a perfect climate, where bananas crops can ripen three or four times a year, and subsidies, means the islanders have the highest beer consumption in the world. They have their own brewery and also drink half of New Zealand's Steinlager.

I stopped there because at the time, returning via Air New Zealand, you could island hop the Pacific at no extra charge and I was interested to learn more about that beautiful place.

Unknowingly, I had booked to arrive in the Cook Islands the week after their triennial Pacific Islands Festival. Interestingly, the New Zealand canoe arrived at the festival a full three months late due to headwinds.

The Cook Islands airport was thatched, and there was nice guitar music in the background. The music stopped and a voice asked, "Aren't you going to applaud?" The music came from a lone guitarist sitting in a tree.

It soon became evident that my hotel car wouldn't be turning up. Fortunately, a baggage van driver called Henry introduced himself and asked if there was a problem. He informed me that his father, uncle, and grandfather had all been prime ministers.

He gave me a lift to the hotel but upon our arrival, we discovered it was closed.

Henry said, rather matter-of-factly, "Ah, that's normal after the Pacific Islands Festival. They've got paralytic drunk and forgotten they have a guest due. I'll take you to our best hotel." It was called The Raratongan Resort Hotel.

It had just begun to rain and I was unnerved to see the rain was draining through the corrugated iron roof into strategically placed buckets. I finally made it to my room and within I discovered a big sign that read: "We are very sorry but there is no room service because we are Pacific Islanders, but we do smile a lot."

In the morning, I opened the shutters and they promptly fell off.

Outside my room was the iconic Pacific island scene: bright sunshine, dazzling, almost white sand, palm trees swaying around a bay, and a reef with waves breaking over it.

I went to breakfast, which was served outside. After half an hour, the waitress appeared, took my order, and disappeared. Half an hour after that, she reappeared and asked if I wanted to order. She took my order and went away again. At least this time she did something useful by shooing the brightly coloured parrots off my table. I soon realised what the problem was when I smelt her breath. Every time, on her way to the kitchen, she had to pass the bar. Apparently, she felt another Steinlager would be a good idea, and subsequently forgot the order.

After breakfast I went to Reception and asked what there was to do. Apparently, Henry also did tours round the island. I asked how long these tours took and was told, "Well, if he drives slowly, about half an hour."

The first thing I saw on my tour was a concrete shell of a large building. I asked my guide what it was, and he answered, "Abandoned. Some years ago, Sheraton decided to build a hotel. We said we don't want it as we can't work to your standard, just like the notice in your room says. They didn't understand what self-government was, so we deported all their workers, and eventually they understood."

Then we looked at some of the trees, whose fruit made everyone self-sufficient throughout the year. Eventually we got to two big patches of burnt sand and I again asked for some background. My guide explained that the first was the site of the prison up until just a week before. A man had been put in prison for his own safety because of a spectacular drinking binge. His jailer was his cousin. They both got drunk in prison and hatched a plan to burn it down.

The plan worked all too well, given that the prison was thatched. As the prison burnt down, a spark caught the roof of the nearby thatched Parliament building, and that burnt down, too.

The oddest thing was that in a country where life was devoted to drinking, Standard Chartered had put up a huge bank, rumoured to contain a lot of monies from tax evasion and money laundering. The natural consequence was that a New Zealand journalist used the promise of gallons of free beer to extract a list of their Standard Chartered's clients on the Cook Islands. This included a number of New Zealand ministers, evading their own taxes.

Of course, nowhere is a paradise other than to tourists who take things at face value. Within a year, the Cook Islands suffered a financial crisis. I also spoke to a white New Zealander who had lived in the Cook Islands for over thirty years and was about to be deported on racial grounds.

Curacao

Curacao is an island in the Caribbean near to Aruba and Bonaire and is within the ABC Islands. The ABC Islands are slightly self-governing parts of the Kingdom of the Netherlands. The self-government was tested recently when a left wing party was elected in Aruba and quadrupled aircraft landing charges. Thrifty KLM said they would not pay and stopped flying there. However, part of the Netherlands to which KLM would not fly was an issue for the Dutch government. So, they decided in favour of KLM. So much for self-governing!

The ABCs are part of the Dutch West Indies, much closer to South America than the British West Indies. In fact, Curacao is in deep water just off Venezuela. This is convenient for Venezuela, because its Lake Maracaibo is a major oil producer, but it is only shallow. Therefore, Venezuela's oil is put into barges on Lake Maracaibo, and barged to Curacao. There it is refined, and put into deep sea tankers for export.

Now, the near-communist Mr Chavez of Venezuela and the American President George W. Bush did not get on. Chavez held a weekly "Hate George W. Bush" session on television. Eventually, this got back to President Bush, who came up with one of his brighter ideas.

"I know," he said, "we'll bomb Venezuela's oil refinery. That'll shut them up."

Nothing came of it, however. The State Department was only vague about Venezuela, and nobody knew Curacao was anything but some sort of a drink.

There was a wing of the US Air Force parked at one end of Curacao's runway, and a wing of the Dutch Air Force at the other end. Presumably, the Dutch had found out from NATO that the US Air Force was about to bomb their refinery.

So, there they were, with George W. not having a clue he was about to declare war on a NATO country by bombing one of its refineries, killing Dutch people in the process. Fortunately, the Dutch are the world's best long-term planners. They had a short-term measure ready. In the middle of the night, when the US planes were in their hangars, the Dutch declared emergency repairs of the runway just outside, and strategically parked a number of bulldozers.

Otherwise, Curacao is a liqueur, which is based on marmalade oranges which were transported there originally by mistake instead of eating oranges. The fruit shrivelled in the intense sun, and somebody found it could be added to spirit to make an excellent liqueur. Beware most of it in circulation is fake, so look for a blue drink in a flattish bottle. The label "Curacao de Curacao" denotes the real thing.

Aruba

How can an island so close to Curacao, be so different? Its ownership is the same, yet, where Curacao is slightly threatening, Aruba is happy. Aruba has a safe environment, compared with ex-British countries, such as St Lucia or Tobago. In Tobago, a tour minibus we took was surrounded by a hostile crowd of drunken male youths because the driver was female and white.

In Aruba everyone has a job. For instance, hotels are not allowed shuttle buses, resulting in lots of jobs for taxi drivers. The island, about the size of the Isle of Man, has 650 restaurants, providing employment. While top-end spending is brought in by cruise liner passengers, Aruba's shops offer genuine savings. For example, an aftershave was 20 per cent cheaper in my hotel than Amsterdam airport's duty free.

Cyprus

A main feature of Cyprus is that it has the same feature as the Isle of Man in that every Cypriot knows all the others. A secretary in one of my employer's firms married a Greek Cypriot from North London.

His family still lived in the rural Troodos Mountains in the centre of the Island. The secretary was in Limassol one time and needed money. This was in the days before cash machines. She went into Barclays and presented a traveller's cheque; but confessed to the cashier, "Oh! I'm sorry. I've forgotten my passport, which I need to cash this."

The cashier, who she had never seen before, and whose name didn't mean anything to her, said, "There is no problem. We heard you were coming, and I'm a second cousin of yours."

This came into its best use later. A rogue employee of a foreign financial services firm conned a foreign millionaire resident in Cyprus out of a huge amount of money. He then skipped the country. Sometime later, he came back when the fuss had died down in order to sell his furniture and get rid of his flat. He did all that, and arranged a night at the Meridien Hotel before flying out the next day.

He believed he had gotten away with everything. Not knowing the island very well, he made a fatal mistake. With checkout at noon, he put the "Do Not Disturb" notice on the handle of his room and left the hotel without paying his bill. This made things totally different. This was stealing money from Greek Cypriots.

When Anna, the room maid, found the guest had scarpered, she rang Anna, the receptionist. She, in turn, rang her cousin Tassos, who ran the airport police. He had the man arrested just as he was boarding his flight out of Cyprus. He received a long prison sentence for robbing a local business. This was entirely clear, whereas what foreigners did amongst themselves with large sums of money was more difficult to determine.

The Cyprus Bailout

Obviously, this story has no jokes attached, because it is a tragedy for the people of the island, who I always found to be very nice.

However, I would like to explain a link with Russia. I have been visiting Cyprus ever since the Cyprus/Turkey war, when the then-Greek Cypriot President, Makarios, declared Enosis, or union with Greece, and the Turkish army stepped in to protect the Turkish third of the population.

For many years there were no Russians, and Cyprus was an upmarket European holiday destination frequented by British and German tourists. My family and I even thought of retiring there.

Suddenly it all changed; the island was flooded with Russians in leather jackets with appalling manners. How did this happen? In all innocence, it was all the fault of the Orthodox Church. It is almost impossible for ordinary Russians to get their money out of Russia. However, the Greek Orthodox and Russian Orthodox churches are almost identical. They helped negotiate the only double tax agreement for Russia with the west, which happened to be between Russia and Cyprus. Russian companies can declare dividends and pay them out to Cyprus.

Lots of Cypriots and small Russian businessmen have lost a great deal in the bailout.

Not so Russians running really big companies. They knew enough to only leave their money in Cyprus for a few seconds then electronically transfer it on to their anonymous and totally safe Swiss bank accounts, leaving nothing in Cyprus

Iceland

Many years after I first visited Iceland in transit, I had occasion to return for a conference. This was a couple of months before they defaulted on their debts. The conference was nothing to do with Iceland itself, but their finance minister insisted on talking to us before the conference started.

He told us, "Don't worry about our liquidity. I've persuaded Norway to prop us up with their oil revenues." He left, and I started the laughter first. Why should Norway do that? It didn't and Iceland went bankrupt.

Compared with my previous visit, they were living beyond their means. All around there was evidence of this with new dual carriageways and a new airport, as just a few examples. These improvements on a big island supported only by the taxes of a quarter million people, was creating public expenditure that didn't add up. The currency was really strong, though. I had to visit a Shell garage for the world's most expensive sandwiches as the hotel restaurant's prices needed a protest.

There was actually no evidence of the Russian mafia who were rumoured to have stolen the money. However, involving them makes the story hang together. Iceland is a tiny country with not enough people regulating a tiny financial services industry. Even in New Zealand, with twelve times the population, regulation of life assurance companies was the part-time job of a clerk in the justice department. There was access under EFTA to all the European Markets. It also explains why Iceland has never been able to return any of the missing money belonging to British and Irish depositors in Icelandic Banks.

Malta

Malta is a very interesting island, from its prehistoric remains to its tunnels under Valetta, which were used for shelter during the Second World War. They speak a very unusual language as well, which is rumoured to be Carthaginian. As Carthage is now Tunis, this is possible. When Scipio Africanus the Younger laid waste to Carthage, he sowed salt on the land, and herded the remaining Carthaginians into a stone quarry to die. It is believed some Carthaginians may have escaped in boats to Malta.

There is evidence of Arabic influence in some of the towns, but nowadays they are all fiercely Catholic. This is shown by the little shrines the bus drivers have on board. They and their passengers need these, given the way they drive on the narrow roads.

The only problem they have is that, having been a British naval base for so long, their cooking has been learnt from the British Navy, so is even more dire than original British before the recent diversification of British society, and thus cooking.

The wine is even worse. This leads me to this old Maltese joke:

The old Maltese winemaker is on his deathbed. He calls for his son and says, "Now that I am dying, I can tell you the most closely guarded secret of Maltese winemaking, which you may only tell your own son on your own deathbed."

"I am listening father," says the son.

"Be prepared for a shock," continued the father, "I have heard wine can also be made from grapes."

I once took a day trip by boat from Malta to Sicily. The saddest things to see were the many abandoned lemon trees. Sicilian lemons are reputed to be the best in the world; but have been priced out of the market by cheap lemons from Morocco.

Recently, I have come across the Knights of Malta, who are the inheritors of the Knights of St John of Jerusalem, or Knights Templar. They are certainly rich, and charitable, and I'm surprised they have not been the subject of a novel by Dan Brown.

Wine

As you, no doubt by now understand, I have travelled a great deal on business. It's not been a bed of roses. I have been to every country I want to go to, and a lot that I didn't. Fortunately, I don't suffer from jet lag. If I could determine why this is, I could bottle it and become a millionaire. However, colleagues who do suffer bad jet lag have copied everything I do, and still end up suffering just as badly. I believe it may have something to do with the fact that on long flights, I naturally sleep a couple of hours, wake for a half hour, and then repeat.

Another thing about business travel is boredom. I found I was giving the same lecture in identical concrete hotels, and then going home tired, and without a sense of having been anywhere new.

Things changed when I had the bright idea of staying on for a couple of days at my own expense and seeing a little bit of the country concerned. That was when I found that half the countries I visited produced wine. By combining my trips with occasional visits to local wineries, I accumulated an amateur and slightly random knowledge of wine.

I bought a huge Eurocave wine storage fridge since it was a lot cheaper than constructing a cellar. The shop did ask if it would be located on concrete on the ground floor since one time they had installed one on the third floor in a flat within an old building. As soon as the owner had filled it with wine, it promptly fell through two floors to the ground.

I bought good quality wine as soon as it was released in order to cellar it for a decade or so. My idea was to store unready wine that would be ready to drink when I retired. Now, once a month or so we enjoy a bottle of wine, whose current prices have become ludicrous.

Chilean Wine

The best example of my interest in wine, and its subsequent ability to free me from stress, occurred in Santiago de Chile.

We had arranged an afternoon meeting, at which the legendary Chilean pensions superintendent would meet the legendarily blunt Dutch pension funds. In the Netherlands, unlike Britain or the US, the Pension Funds are arranged by Union or trade, and membership is compulsory for everyone in work. Thus they are large, and in the Dutch fashion, do everthing in groups Like other Dutch people, they are very blunt in the way they talk, with no pleasantries. The talk was due to begin at 2.00 p.m. To give us time to prepare, we had booked the hotel conference room for the entire day.

When we arrived, the hotel had double-booked the room during the morning and lunchtime to another company, and wouldn't give us access. This was despite the fact that we could show confirmation of our booking for the morning.

I was beginning to panic about what would go wrong since we now couldn't prepare. I took a deep breath, went to reception, and asked if there was a winery near enough to visit that would enable me to come back by 12:30 p.m. We were in luck, there was one—it happened to be Chile's oldest winery, Cosino Macul. I took a taxi and had a very good morning without worrying about the conference. I tasted their finest wine Finis Terrae, which translates to Ends of the Earth. I thought this was most appropriate for Chile, since it is the most southern country and the nearest to the Antarctic.

I got back to the hotel at 12.30 p.m., managed to get entry to the room we had booked by 1.15 p.m., and found, as I had feared, an organisational shambles. The hotel had tacked the company flag to the front of the dais table. However, they only had roving microphones with leads, and they had tacked all of them behind the flag. This created a situation whereby the microphones could not have been used and nobody would be able to hear any of the audience questions. The screen had been set up for left-handed people. The floors were covered by loose cables, making it very likely that speakers would fall over if they moved to the screen.

Fortunately, the hotel staff worked quickly to my instructions. Also, as the Chilean superintendent was a well-known speaker, the simultaneous translators of Spanish to English (which all the Dutch attendees spoke), were well up to speed. They had questions for me because our document had been translated from my English to Spanish by someone who spoke Spanish but did not know pensions. He had made the mistake of translating the English word *annuity*, which is a monthly payment, into *annuario*, which means an annual payment.

Conflict Between the Chilean and Dutch Views of Social Justice

After all that, there came a fascinating exchange of incompatible viewpoints. The Dutch are very keen on social justice. Because commissions were regulated to a low level in Chile, the financial intermediaries were moving their clients' monies lots of times between different funds to collect lots of introductory commissions.

The Dutch group said to the Chilean Pensions Superintendant: "We have heard your intermediaries are ripping off (actual words) the man in the street by churning funds. What do you propose to do about it?"

The Chilean Superintendent replied: "Well, you see we have a capitalist economy here. In capitalism, if you are stupid, you get ripped off. So, we will do nothing."

Old World Wines

Back to wine. I am frequently asked if I prefer European or New World wines. As far as I'm concerned, you can't compare them.

They are made according to different philosophies. Few people know one major difference is the tax regime. After vinification, the wine stays for some time in oak casks in Europe to mature and take on some flavour from the wood, because tax is levied when it it taken from the barrel. In contrast, since wine is taxed when it goes into the barrel in the New World, the wine is made to mature much earlier than in the Old World.

The Company Secretary of Penfolds

Most Australian wines are made to mature quickly in order to create uniformity of taste. On a flight, I once sat next to the company secretary of Penfolds, Australia's biggest wine producer.

I asked her, "How do you get the magnificent constant oak taste in your chardonnays, given the variability of oak barrels?"

She laughed and said, "Barrels? Barrels? We mature in huge stainless steel vats, and wave oak chippings up and down in them for a standard time, Mate."

The Company Secretary of Schweppes, Australia

I also once travelled next to the Company Secretary of Schweppes. I felt quite sorry for the Qantas crew since that airline did not stock Schweppes, and she vociferously wanted to know why on a flight that lasted approximately about three hours.

French Classified Growths—The Top of the Pyramid

At the pinnacle of wine production in France are the "crus classifies", or the classified growths. This system was developed in France in the Bordeaux region, or claret region, in the mid-nineteenth century, and copied elsewhere in France.

The lowest classification is "AOC" or Appellation d'Ordinaire Controlee, which says the wine was made within the traditional boundaries of the Bordeaux region. A good way above this classification is Bordeaux Superior.

Top of the quality spectrum, are the 58 Grand Crus. The problem with the classification system is that it is in six ranks. That was how the wines tasted in the mid-nineteenth century, but is not relevant now. Only one wine has ever changed classification. Mouton Rothschild went from second rank to first. This is rumoured to have cost the French Rothschilds almost all their money.

The Chinese Influence on Wine Prices

There is the recent legend that Chateau Lafite is the world's best wine. This is a gross oversimplification. All the first growths taste slightly different. The verdict on Lafite is based on price. Its price is based on the fact it is the only one of the five wines that bears a name that the Chinese can pronounce.

Another example of the influence the Chinese hold on the wine market is the sudden rise in price of Chateau Beycheville.

This has an interesting story. King Henry IV gave his favourite courtier a vineyard on the river that runs through Bordeaux, made him the Duc d'Epernon, then went on to make him Lord High Admiral of France. Since the courtier now owned a winery by the River Gironde and was High Admiral, all the ships passing the vineyard on the river had to lower their sails as they passed in respect. In French, the term "lower the sails" is "baisser les voiles", which became corrupted to "Beychevelle".

The wine label is of a sailing ship with the sails lowered. The Chinese saw this, and called it Dragon Boat wine. This has caused a huge increase in the price.

The problem about demand from China and South East Asia is that so many people, many of whom are missing the chromosome that enables them to enjoy alcohol, are now trying to drink the number one wines at the same time.

Many years ago, I met a man in what was then the Berry Brothers wine shop at Terminal Four at Heathrow. He had just bought six bottles of Chateau Latour at an enormous price. I remarked that it looked as though he would be having some party. He said he worked for a phenomenally rich cement manufacturer in Thailand. Each week, the richest billionaires in Thailand got together for dinner. It was a BYOB party (bring your own bottle), but, because of who they were, the bottle had to be the number one bottle.

This, and similar events amongst the other muli millionaires of South East Asia explains the demand for Premier Cru Bordeaux. I asked the man how they were able to taste the subtle flavours through the heat of Thai cuisine, and he answered that he was not sure, apart from their palates being accustomed to the heat. But, he did say he'd heard the rumour that some drank their wine mixed with Coca Cola. I have no problem with this with ordinary wine, but it's a bit off with wines of huge scarcity.

Outstanding Wines

The good thing about the Chinese buying wine at ridiculous prices is that they only use the 1852 classification for determining the best wines. I would have to say that there isn't actually a best wine. There are a couple of dozen outstanding wines and not all from France.

Beyond the five premier crus, I personally would add: Ch Palmer (Bordeaux). Many reckon it would be reclassified as Premier Cru nowadays if they revised the classification; and their second wine (made from younger vines than used in the main wine) is Alter Ego de Palmer, also exceptionally good.

Ornellia and Sassiacaia are the original Italian super Tuscans. The term is now debased, but these two are first class Chiantis with a mix of other grapes like Cabernet. Vega Sicilia Unico from Spain, Hill of Grace, and Grange from Australia, are also wines of the quality of the premier cru Bordeaux. So are various garage wines in the US, such as Screaming Eagle. Garage wines are wines made to incredible standards in tiny quantities, often with Silicon Valley money.

US Wines

America does not yet understand the balance between production and quality which is understood so well in Australia, though all of these matters are improving. It is interesting that the millennium party for top chardonnay makers was not in France, but at Sonoma Cutrer, the magnificent new winery in the hills above the Napa Valley. It must have Silicon Valley money behind it, and the only advertising is to host the annual world croquet championship. They claim they cut the croquet lawns by laser. Even if not true, it looks as if they do.

Put these together and there are plenty of wines around the world of equal quality to the French premier cru at cheaper prices.

I deliberately exclude Burgundy because it is much more complicated. The vineyards are tiny because of Burgundian inheritance laws. Also, I don't like it. You are ether a Bordeaux or Burgundy person.

So there we have a recap of the old traditional world. Things become more complicated when you buy cheap wines from the Old World, because they use many of the New World techniques, which they can do in parts of France that are not subject to production rules.

Robert Parker

To show palates are individual, the greatest wine critic, Robert Parker, scores wines from one to one hundred, and does not like New Zealand reds because he says they taste of cabbage, or something like that.

I, on the other hand, think the boutique wines, made in the warmer environment of Waiheke Island, in the Hauraki Gulf of New Zealand, are outstanding. One of them is Peninsula. I saw it spelled as Peninsular on a restaurant menu, and told them they had a problem. They replied, "No, we have two problems. The other one is we don't have any."

New World Wine Technology

The use of technology is key in the New World. I have already mentioned abandoning oak cask maturation for waving a bag of oak chips up and down in a stainless steel vat. Grapes are pressed with modern presses in which the grapes are actually pressed by an airbag, to prevent damage Techniques like refining the wine by using a sediment of eggshells (still used by a handful of classified growers in Bordeaux), are long gone.

The technology is used to bring the customer the taste he wants. A few years ago a British Airways blind taste selected New Zealand Sauvignon for their international traveller class. The problem is this meant it had to be bottled in quarter bottles and New Zealand did not have a quarter bottle bottling line. The Kiwis and BA agreed that BA would buy the wine in quarter sized bottles until a line to bottle quarter bottles had been paid for, thus giving certainty to the winemakers to spend a lot of money on a new product. This is a good example of working with customers.

New Zealand—Cloudy Bay Wine

Many people may have heard of this wine. It was the first sauvignon blanc not to taste boring. The taste in the mouth goes on much longer than French examples of sauvignon, and there is also a taste of asparagus, grass, and gooseberry.

This is only possible in the New World because there are no enforced rules on how to produce the wine.

The Cloudy Bay climate is on the fringe for making this variety of wine, which means the grapes are stressed, which normally produces better wines. Because the climate in Marlborough is variable, half the grapes are grown in the open air and half under the shade of netting. If frost threatens bud setting, a helicopter is hired from Marlborough airport and a weather balloon is sent up. If it shows frosty air descending, the helicopter goes to that height and blows the cold air away like a giant fan.

When harvest time rolls around, a mass spectrometer is used to mix the sunshine and shaded grapes to produce exactly the same taste as the previous year.

I one went into the old Tesco Vins at Calais. Cloudy Bay was shown on the premium wines list, but there wasn't any available. The French assistant explained they had it in the back, but were not putting it on sale. They explained further that to say a New Zealand wine was good, was an insult to France.

I asked him to read the label properly, because after Cloudy Bay won first prize in Paris, the French Government closed the competition to foreigners in future. They also ordered Pernod Ricard to buy Cloudy Bay and restrict production. When the assistant read the label and realised Cloudy Bay was indeed owned by Pernod Ricard, he was full of apologies and brought out an entire case for me.

By the way, technology is also used in some red wines. I have heard that Grange, the Australian super red, uses some extract of walnut skin in the process.

British Airways and Wine as Compared with Some Other Airlines

British Airways and wine is an interesting subject because British Airways takes wine seriously, unlike most airlines. As an example of the latter, a recent long haul business class flight on KLM brought a novel way of selecting good wines. They were all Dutch wines from vineyards owned by the Dutch, or where the winemaker was Dutch. There is actually no connection between good wines and Dutch-ness. I had certainly not even heard of any of the wines, and was quite glad I hadn't.

A more common mistake is made by many airlines from America. They choose premier or deuxieme cru wines (first or second clas in the 1852 classification of Bordeaux wines) for their premium class passengers. Unfortunately, these tend to be heavily tannic (tasting of black, unsweetened tea). The effect of tannin is much greater at height, so many of the less famous wines are better because, strangely, the cabin pressure accentuates the tannin taste.

In contrast, British Airways uses Masters of Wine to do the penultimate selection. Masters of Wine have been taught how to allow for this change in taste due to height and pressure. A panel of wine experts produce two winners for each category of wine (e.g., red, heavy, and business class). At that stage, the final selection moves to buying to get the best deal for a single wine to be offered on board in each category.

I did a wonderful tour of Bordeaux, via the BA Executive Club, with their head of wine. He was a former first class steward who had followed through his interest in wine by taking exams. Because I can speak French, I helped him translate when he got stuck.

In St Emilion, which is part of the Bordeaux vineyards, we dined at a restaurant with a very long wine list. It consisted entirely of all the wines of St Emilion. There was only one entry under the heading "Vins Etrangeres" (foreign wines). This was a Côtes du Rhône. Not exactly how we would designate a foreign wine, but it shows how passionate the French are about their own locality.

Sauternes—Sweet Wines

The best vineyard visit was to Chateau Nairac, owned by the well-known Mme Taari. We had dinner there as well, and every course was accompanied by a different vintage of this sweet wine, apart from the roquefort, which was served with a Chateau Nairac claret. The Nairac sweet wine is described as Barsac/Sauternes, because the winery is in one of the appellations and the vines are in the other.

We arrived while it was bucketing with rain and with dubious lighting. The owner warned us to "beware of the poodles."

My questioning of the recipe for the excellent chicken liver pie was naturally answered with, "I do not know. Ze little man from ze village brings it on his bicyclette."

However, I got my own back because she considered the simplified wine vintage classification in my diary was the best simple classification she had seen, and she was going to write to Hermes and ask them to put it in their diaries.

An Unscheduled Stop—The Lesson of Buying Power

To conclude our tour, we made an unscheduled stop at a vineyard which was not on our list. The man from BA said he had heard their white wine was improving greatly, and he would like to taste it.

It took a while, but eventually someone opened the door. We could see everyone at lunch while the man from the vineyard glanced at the business card and declared in French, "Get lost. We don't take tour buses, you idiots," and started to slam the door.

I stuck my foot in the door, and explained in French that, if he'd bothered to read the business card, he would see this man was the chief wine buyer of British Airways. The penny still didn't drop.

I then explained the Englishman personally was the largest buyer of classified Bordeaux in the world. Everything changed in an instant. He yelled at his staff and then said in hesitant English to the man from BA, "Ah! I did not understand until le monsieur explained. Come in and share our 'umble lunch of bread and wine. You are welcome to taste as much of any wine you want that we make."

The Napa Valley

I also went on a very interesting week-long wine tour in the Napa and Sonoma Valleys, north of San Francisco. It was a clear demonstration that wine can be made without regard to the local characteristics, or "terroir", so beloved of the French. Most US vineyards make both red and white in the same area.

There was sheer amazement in the hotel at Calistoga Spa Hot Springs when I got a call from foreign (i.e., my office). Apparently, the hotel staff didn't know we spoke English in England. The trip was an amazing tasting of wines made differently than Europe.

John Duval

I did a tour of Yosemite after the wine tour in California. John Duval, then the chief winemaker of Penfolds, was also on the bus. He had found the US market polarized between the low quality jug wines and the super high quality, but very small, garage wines. This was giving him an opportunity to develop the mid markets for his Australian wines.

Now he has his own brand.

White Wine

Sulphites

Unlike some red wines, whites don't keep. In fact, almost all white wines contain sulphites to enable them to last at all. I had a neighbour in New Zealand who got bad headaches from drinking white wines. I suspected an allergy to sulphites was to blame. I finally found a wine shop that had a Chablis (unoaked chardonnay) from a very traditional and expensive maker who guaranteed no sulphites. My neighbour didn't get a headache after drinking this bottle.

The vast majority of white wines today are dry. Only a couple of generations ago, almost the only white wines drunk were German and sweet. The slowness of the Germans to realise tastes were changing has damaged German wine sales immensely. The Australians have proved you can make dry wines anywhere, including the searing heat of the Clare Valley, which runs up to the edge of the "red centre" of Australia.

A small proportion of very sweet white wines are made and it needs unusual conditions. Most sweet white is made from dry grapes, left until they go mouldy, but harvested before frost. The best is reckoned to be Bordeaux's Chateau d'Yquem.

I visited what the wine guide in New Zealand said was a vineyard making a spectacular sweet wine. When I said to the winemaker that I would like to try some of his sweet wine, he countered with, "So would I. I haven't had the right autumn weather for five years to make any." This just shows how difficult it is.

Canadian Ice Wine

Canadian wines were a bit of a joke until they discovered the influence of the various microclimates of the Great Lakes that exist at different heights, coupled with the influence of Niagara Falls. Also, they went one step beyond Sauternes, and they actually allow the grapes to freeze.

To give a clue to the premium pricing of ice wine, it takes the grapes that would make ten bottles of chardonnay to make one bottle of Sauterne, and the grapes to make ten bottles of Sauterne, to make one bottle of ice wine. If the winemaker is lucky, a bunch of frozen ice wine grapes will produce one drop of wine.

When ice wine was invented, the French declared it was not a wine. Import into Europe was forbidden until some of the manufacturers said they were French Canadian, and the prohibition was immediately lifted.

I once, for fun, asked an assistant at Singapore airport duty free why Icewine was more expensive than Sauternes. She said "because it is better." I asked why was it better? She said because it was more expensive. Ah, the culture of the Far East is now money—Confucius would blush if he was still alive.

Austria—The Sweet Wine Scandal

So, there you have the great sweet whites. However, one of the greatest scandals occurred with the sweet whites of Austria. These can only be produced in tiny quantities due to the climate being marginal. However, at one point there was a vast increase in demand. It was subsequently discovered that in order to meet this demand, the growers had been diluting the wine with antifreeze.

This could not have happened in the controlled wine areas of France, because the methods of growing and production are regularly inspected by the Baillis (freemen who are the other wine producers of each appellation) to ensure all growers adhere to the traditional methods of production.

The Middle East

Abu Dhabi

We spent 1979—81 in Abu Dhabi whilst the city was still being built. Now it is nearly finished, and has probably more modern skyscrapers than New York.

One night there was a fire alarm in my block of flats. I and my colleagues staggered down in our dressing gowns. Meanwhile, the wife of the Japanese businessman in the flat below emerged having dressed in a full kimono.

Fire was quite worrisome in the older buildings, as there were no actual street addresses To solve the problem of post, and for security reasons, all post was delivered to PO boxes rented by one's employer. There were no actual street addresses. Thus you had to try to explain to the fire brigade where you were. Occasionally, you would see fire engines going round and round until they could find smoke.

(Incidentally, the fastest evacuation I ever saw during a fire alarm was in an office in Kazakhstan. Everybody got out before the security guards, who put live ammunition into their Kalashnikovs before they made their rounds to make sure the office was empty.)

Banking

The Banks followed British Indian procedure, which, in general, required two hours plus forty signatures to cash a cheque. My Belgian colleague introduced me to ABN AMRO. In pre-computer days, the bank manager had an entirely practical Dutch-type solution. He employed an Indian lady with a photographic memory, who remembered the balances of all the customers. Cashing a cheque took only a couple of minutes. ABN, before the banking disaster, was an interesting bank in that the authority of the manager to make changes such as that depended on the amount of trust the Chairman had in him.

Travel

Because we lived away from London in those days, and you could guarantee the newly merged British Airways, or Heathrow, would lose your luggage, we flew via Amsterdam on KLM. Their flights to Abu Dhabi were via Jeddah, where everyone had to dispose of all alcohol before the religious police searched the aircraft.

On one flight, there were a large number of labourers on board, whom I took to be possibly Indonesian. They were making the Haj, or pilgrimage, to Mecca. They didn't speak English or Dutch; and early in the flight, they took out a primus stove, and started pumping the pressure in the aisle before cooking their dinner. At that stage, we were glad the Dutch are usually quite big, because the stewardesses wrestled them to the ground, sat on them, and put them in handcuffs.

Carpets

When we first arrived, I was with one of my colleagues who happened to be shopping for carpets for his flat. He asked the shop assistant if he had any Omani carpets. The assistant took him to a pile of English-style carpets. My colleague pointed out to the assistant that, unfortunately, those were not Omani carpets. The assistant argued, "Yes they are. I show." He turned over the label, which was clearly marked, "Romanian". "See," he said, "Omani."

Groceries

The first proper grocery shop I went into in Abu Dhabi was very small. I looked for baked beans, and only found one tin. I took it and put it in my basket. When I turned round, I saw another tin in its place. "What new technology is this?" I thought.

I took the second tin, but this time I watched. A hand came from behind the shelf and put another tin in its place!

Der Cooling Down

It was seriously hot in the summer, when I lived in Abu Dhabi. Temperatures reached a soaring 145F (a whopping 62.8C)! For my day off, we joined the pool club of the newly built Sheraton. The pool was set in concrete, surrounded by tables and chairs with waiter service from the hotel.

You could recognise the members of the pool club because we were all very brown, wearing flip-flops, and approached the pool carefully. Pool club members would then sit on the edge of the pool and lower themselves in slowly. This was necessary because of the contrast between the air temperature of 145F, and that of the pool at 100F.

On one occasion, I noticed two young German businessmen were being unpleasant to the Sheraton staff. I found this to be particularly unkind considering the staff's tiny wages and the amount of time they had to spend outside in the heat. However, I also watched as the Germans ran in their bare feet across the concrete, and jumped straight into the pool. Running across the concrete would serve them right, because they would develop huge blisters on the soles of their feet due to the extreme heat.

When they entered the water, one yelled to the other, "Ach, der cooling down." They didn't realise how lucky they were. They must have been perfectly fit, because they didn't have an immediate heart attack.

The conclusion to draw from this would be to take it slowly and observe the ways of a strange country so you do not cause offence and do not get into trouble. Even today there are some idiots from England who do not realise that in a Muslim country like Dubai you should be discreet if you are allowed to drink alcohol.

Red Wine Mixed with White is the Ultimate Offence to a Winemaker

I was having dinner with a German count in the Sheraton hotel. He was also a distinguished winemaker.

Dinner was at the hotel because only hotels were licenced to serve alcohol, and then, only under strict conditions, such as only to non-Muslim westerners. At the time, the Sheraton had breached the rules, and so, was in the process of having its licence revoked.

The waiter said there were only two bottles of wine left in the hotel. I had to explain this to the winemaker, because he had started looking at the wine list. It was only a choice of red or white, one bottle of each available, and, of course, no choice of vineyard.

We drank the red first. The winemaker then asked the waiter to bring the other bottle. The waiter was from Pakistan, an officially dry country, so by definition, he knew nothing at all about wine.

When he returned, our glasses of red were still a quarter full, but apparently unconcerned about this, the waiter opened the bottle of white, and poured it into the red.

I can still remember the look of horror on the winemaker's face.

The winemaker took me to dinner in Munich when I was visiting for a conference and as we drove around, we came across the town hall. He said his town house had once been there, until it was bombed flat by the British. That was difficult to respond to but what made it even worse, was that I was aware his father had been another Schindler, smuggling out Jews via his other estate in Hungary.

I didn't know what to say.

He died young, so rest in peace, Manfred. He was one of the good guys.

The Netherlands

The Rudest Country in Europe

I also worked for the Dutch. They speak a language that they refer to as *Dutch Direct*, but I would call it rude. They are the rudest and most puffed up people in Europe. "God made the world, but the Dutch made the Netherlands" refers to the fact that a third of the Netherlands is reclaimed land. The frequent winter fog at Schiphol Airport is due to the fact that three centuries ago, it was sea.

I once asked a Dutchman why mobile phone reception was so good in the Netherlands and appalling in Norfolk, given both were equally flat. He replied, "Because we build our mobile phone masts twice as high as you do, because you are stupid." The first half of that sentence is informative. The second is gratuitous rudeness.

I asked another Dutchman why their English is near perfect. He answered, "We all watch BBC TV, because you are stupid enough to give us reception free of the licence fee."

Recently, I was boarding a train in Amsterdam when the guard closed the doors on me. He came round later to say that next time he would rip my leg off with the door. And it is the Dutch who are supposed to be teaching the staff on Greater Anglia Rail, who are already very polite, how to be polite.

Eating Habits

Eating is incredibly plain at ABN AMRO, with lunch being exactly the same every day. It was a plain ham sandwich, a plain cheese sandwich, and a glass of milk. Once, the kitchen served fresh raw herring in one of the sandwiches. This is their favourite food. Paradoxically, there were lots of complaints that the unexpected filling had disturbed concentration in meetings, and the kitchen was not to do it again.

In the canteen, you had to unload your own tray. The first time, I didn't understand the system, and put a fork in the container for dirty knives. The Indonesian kitchen assistant behind the hatch swore at me loudly in English which involved copious use of the F word.

The most popular food in the canteen was a meatball on a slice of bread.

If you visit a Dutch home, it will only be by prior invitation, and you will be served a small cup of coffee, and one small biscuit only.

Drug Culture: Company Time and Private Time

Contrary to public perception, drugs are not legal in the Netherlands. Smoking them comes under the general rules of private time and company time. During company time, you work short hours very intensively and your time belongs to your company. During private time, your time belongs to yourself. You can do whatever you like as long as you do not offend others substantially in public.

As far as drugs are concerned, once there was a police notice in all hotel rooms. It said "Do not buy drugs on the street. The white powder is baking powder and the seller's accomplice will steal your wallet."

This is a good example of practical advice, which is much better than threats.

The British Investment Banker and the Thirty-five Hour Week

An example of the British not understanding private time was illustrated by a UK investment banker on assignment in the Dutch head office. Upon starting his assignment, he was given his time clock, which also opened the security turnstiles. Thinking of his bonus, he worked fifteen hours on Monday, fifteen on Tuesday, and six hours until lunch on Wednesday. He then had to attend a lunchtime meeting at another bank.

When he came back, his time clock would not give him access through the security gates. He assumed it was faulty, and complained to the receptionists. They explained that he had already done thirty-six hours that week. He responded with, "So what? I work until the job is done."

"Not here," said the receptionists, "There is a legal maximum of thirty-five hours a week. You have done more than that and now you have to go home for your private time until the time clock admits you again."

"When will that be?" asked the banker.

"Monday morning. Then it will only admit you for thirty-four hours in the week, deducting your illegal extra hour this week."

No wonder investment bankers work from London or New York. Due to the short hours permitted in the Netherlands, the banker lost the deal.

Germany—The Same Idea

Germany has the same idea. A friend ran a Reuters bank computer trading systems repair team when he was younger. One of the major German banks' trading systems crashed on a Friday afternoon. Believe me when I say it was a major crash. The team took the next plane from Heathrow, to camp in the bank's offices until Monday morning to get the system working for the new trading week.

They arrived at 5.00 p.m. on Friday. At 7.30 p.m., a man told them to get out until Monday morning because the bank was closing for the weekend. They explained if they did that, the bank would lose millions of Euros. The man said he was the union convenor, and that he would not let them work in contravention of the legal time clock rules. Besides which, the lights and electricity would switch of at 8.00 p.m., and the outside doors would shut.

Subsequently, and as predicted, the bank lost millions.

Thrift

The Dutch are allotted huge amounts of holiday time, but have no money because they also pay huge taxes to support huge social benefits. Therefore, they clutter up roads throughout Europe in the summer with their caravans.

We were once travelling the wonderful single track road round the Ring of Kerry in Ireland. At one point, we found ourselves stuck behind an oil tanker making a delivery. To our surprise and delight, a lady came out from a nearby house with cups of tea for us. That is legendary Irish hospitality.

Later on, we were behind a couple of Dutch caravans travelling at an achingly slow five mph. Eventually, we came to a folk museum. To our dismay, the caravans pulled in ahead of us.

I told my companions not to worry because the Dutch people would merely look at the postcards, discuss them, and decide they have seen what there is to see, so don't need a purchase a reminder. Besides, the scenes wouldn't mean anything to their friends. As it turns out, it happened just that way.

This attitude to postcards explains why over half of those I posted to the UK from Amsterdam never arrived. The Dutch were happy to take the money for postage, but thought people were stupid to send them to others who had never seen the sights on the postcards, so they couldn't be interested in receiving them.

The Rood Light

When a Dutch train stops between stations, and the guard announces, "Die trein am stopped aan die rood licht," does it mean the train has stopped at a red light, or the train has stopped to let people off for the red light district? The red light district is another example of what you can do in your private time!

Brazil

Safety on the Street

Brazil is an amazing country. For a start, apart from rural China, it is the country with the largest number of people who don't speak English. Secondly, it has a high crime rate. This is true in Sao Paolo, where I did most of my business.

For example, you are booked into a hotel close to the office you are visiting, and you are given instructions how to walk, e.g., in the middle of the street.

If you have need of a taxi, you are told your hotel or office must order it for you; because as a person who neither speaks Brazilian Portuguese, nor looks Brazilian, you won't be able to hail one yourself.

To ensure your safety in getting to your destination, they will give instructions to the driver and write down the number of the cab. I thought I was very clever in learning the Portuguese for please give me a receipt, but the taxi driver burst out laughing. I asked my colleagues who met the cab what was so funny. They explained that my Portuguese was correct for Portugal, but in Brazil, where the right wording was, "Scribble me a note of the fare," my Portuguese sounded like "Will you make me up a book of accounting, please?"

Traffic and Hotels

Sao Paolo is a huge sprawling city. Out of necessity, traffic comes to a standstill when it rains, because somebody stole the money earmarked to build an underground flood chamber for the central motorway. Therefore, when it rains, the motorway is covered in bright orange water from the river.

The advice for hotels is to book into the most recently built. Once they age, they suffer from local standards of repair.

Once, getting back into my room the early morning after a long session of first rate hospitality, I stumbled and fell against a mirror which was covering a whole wall. Surprisingly, the mirror actually opened, revealing a big cupboard. On the left were water pipes, and on the right, a mass of wiring. The wires were joined by bare wires being wound together. As well, the plumbing constantly issued small jets of water. And that was a five star hotel operated by one of the big American chains!

Rio de Janeiro

To me, Rio is a really scary place. This is because the mountains, the slums, the business district, and the middle class housing, are all thrown together in a way that does not happen elsewhere In Brazil, because Rio's geography of high mountains near the beaches mean all types of residents live closely together. It is the only place I had a minder, who was a huge Brazilian-speaking American ex-linebacker. I was grateful he was there.

Brasilia

I found Brasilia to be an artificial city, with some ideas which probably seemed a good idea when the City was built in the 1960's but seem odd now. Everything was zoned, so all the hotels were together. The set up for a bathroom was that it was a room with only a sink, a loo, and a tiled floor with a drain in the middle. Bathing or showering involved using a shower attachment which was joined to the loo. In order to operate it, one must turn a valve, flush the loo, and out would come a shower of cold water!

Before visiting Brasilia, I was told there would probably be someone who spoke English. There wasn't. After my arrival, I was told the point of my presence was to assist the bank's Brasilia bank manager, who had started his career washing floors in the bank, in his endeavours to show senior people from their central bank and the gas company that the bank now had foreign experts.

When I returned to Britain, I was asked my opinion of Brazilian women, particularly when they were on the beach. I said that in my opinion, they were unhealthily thin. For about six months afterwards, every time I entered the London office, I received a chorus of, "Benny Hill, Benny Hill."

Argentina

I had an Irish grandfather who was born in Northern Ireland before partition. Therefore, I was able to procure an Irish passport, which would ease travelling in difficult countries. Everyone from the BA London flight was being frisked. But when I held up my Irish passport, I was cheered by the customs staff and got an immediate green light.

The Iguacu Falls, drain the lower Amazon rainforest at the meeting point of Argentina, Brazil, and Paraguay. How does one decide which country they are entering? At the Argentine border, the guards cheered at the Irish passport. At the Brazilian border, they were asleep. At Paraguay's border, which I gather is a duty free country, there was nobody there.

Russia

Tangle with the Russian Mafia at your own peril; both Iceland, and now Cyprus, have found that out the hard way.

So much of Russian business is controlled by the Mafia. Russian vodka is not pure odourless spirit like western vodka, but has many contaminants which make it very dangerous and smelly (I assume the Russian vodka as exported is safe.)which is why it smells. Grand Metropolitan/Diageo thought this would be a good chance to put up a plant to brew pure Stolichnaya. They ignored the mafia warnings, and their chief executive was mysteriously shot.

The Mafia controlled furniture manufacture when Ikea built a shop in Russia. They were controlled more elegantly than the vodka distillers. When I went past their new store, there was only one car in the car park, right in the middle. It was a Volvo which had been thoroughly machine-gunned.

Snow on the Pea Soup

A Scottish friend who was a fishing nut asked me about a fishing trip to Russia he had been offered, which was located in the middle of nowhere. I explained that he would probably be introduced to some men in black leather jackets. He should pay them an agreed price in new dollar notes. He would then be taken to a bendy river. The Mafia would organise the people in the local village. Half would put fish round the bend upstream of him. The other half would retrieve the fish he had not caught round the bend downstream of him. When all was said and done, he would agree with his friends who had recommended the trip that it was his best fishing ever.

New Zealand: Lateral Thinking on the Topics of Defence and the Riches of the Seas

I lived in New Zealand. They are a long way from anywhere. Australia calls New Zealand its East Island, but it isn't. It is actually four hours away by plane, which is akin to the distance between London and Cyprus. It is a mainly Presbyterian country. It is also home to the Maoris, who are conscious they are the only local inhabitants in the world that the British could not defeatin battle in the nineteenth century Beware criticising anything at all. The locals consider they live in God's own country, shortened to the term, "Godzone".

The distance away meant almost nil expenditure on their armed forces. Australia, with its first class army, would be attacked first. In Serbia, the New Zealand contingent asked to borrow some British Warrior armoured cars, since theirs dated back to Vietnam.

Their best military effort was at sea. They only had three World War II era ex-British coal-burning destroyers. They steamed in a line across the Gulf of Auckland every day in a show of force, not letting on that the middle ship was on tow because its engine had been replaced by concrete.

Why, then, you might ask, did the Polish trawlers that were illegally fishing New Zealand's pristine waters, cut their nets and retreat at full speed, when they saw the black smoke on the horizon signalling that a New Zealand destroyer was heading for them?

Well, the answer begins with Greenpeace being at the centre of New Zealand politics. If the destroyers had fired their ancient guns, they would probably have exploded.

Instead, before sailing their Navy phoned Greenpeace to say there were trawlers pillaging the seas. The Navy loaded the destroyer with Greenpeace inflatables and protesters. When they got near enough to the offending trawler, they released the Greenpeace members. The trawlers concerned never did it again.

Another wonderful incident occurred when the Marks &Spencer store chain buyers visited New Zealand to buy fish without telephoning beforehand. This happened a few years ago at the height of M&S's arrogance. (For example, whilst in their store if you asked for help, a snooty assistant would respond with a discourteous, "No," and walk away.)

The store chain buyers knew their beverage colleagues bought wine without any problem. What they did not know was that the winemakers were in hoots of laughter about the M&S wines. One winemaker related that they were given very detailed instructions on how to make the M&S wines. These instructions were drawn up by people who had previously been ladies underwear buyers. The winemakers said these instructions produced wine tasting of "cat's pee on a gooseberry bush". In this way, M&S wine sales did not impact on sales of wine produced to the winemaker's own production criteria.

Back to the M&S fish buyers: They found that the biggest NZ fishing company was not interested, and the second biggest was Maori. This meant they were talking at cultural cross purposes because the Maori are a people whose society is not based on money.

Finally though, the finance director of the third biggest fishery, agreed to see them in his modest hut in Auckland Harbour. They arrogantly presented their demand for a certain amount of Orange Roughy, the tastiest and most highly prized fish in, possibly, the world. They also presented their demands for specific delivery times, as well as the price they were willing to pay.

The New Zealander gently explained the ecological management of New Zealand waters. He said the entire landing of Orange Roughy was airlifted immediately after being caught and packed in ice to Japan where it was eaten as sushi. There was a little spare Hoki, however, (which New Zealanders considered cat food). He then enquired as to whether M&S would be paying the fishing company's set price in dollars, deutschmarks, or yen, because they did not accept weak currencies like sterling.

No story about New Zealand is complete without one about the sheepdogs. In the South Island mountains, called the Southern Alps, they used to bring the mountain sheep out of the hills by using horses. Now, however, they use the sound of helicopters. When on the plains, there can be herds of sheep numbering in the tens of thousands. They are able to herd these with a collie and a second dog—a huge crossbreed called a Huntaway. The Huntaway is a stupid dog, but he barks very loudly at the back of the huge herd of sheep to keep them moving. Meanwhile, the very intelligent collie is trained to run over the backs of the sheep, rather than around them.

Sri Lanka—A Hotel's Old-Fashioned Bell Pull

I visited Sri Lanka many years ago. Breakfast usually consisted of egg hoppers—pancakes containing an egg and vindaloo sauce. I can still remember the shock.

One evening, I asked where the minibar was located and was told they were a poor country so they didn't have one. It was suggested, however, that if I pulled the old-fashioned rope by the bed, a butler would come and provide anything I wanted.

During our visit, we hired a car with driver to go into the interior and visit the old capital, Kandy. The car was a Morris Minor of great antiquity, with the doors held on by string. I could see that halfway up the steep road to Kandy, all the cars were stopping. On closer inspection it seemed that a stream had been dammed to feed a hosepipe, and all the cars were refilling their radiators.

Sweden and the Behaviour of the Japanese Royal Household

I visited Sweden quite a lot on business and stayed at the Grand Hotel, Stockholm, across the harbour from the Royal Palace. It is interesting to note that Nobel Prize laureates and their families have all been guests at that hotel.

On one occasion, the Japanese Emperor was also visiting Sweden. There were not enough vacancies at the Japanese embassy, so many Japanese royal retainers were staying at the Grand. The juniors carried umbrellas for the seniors, and they all came down in the lift strictly in order of seniority.

One junior panicked that he had forgotten something, and scurried back to the lift. Unfortunately, he got into a lift where two seniors were getting out. There were audible hisses from all the Royal retainers present. There was a look of terror on his face, before two beefy seniors physically picked him up and took him away.

Italy, the Bella Signorina in the Carabinieri—Only in Italy

The Chinese president was staying in Milan at the same hotel I was staying for a conference. The Caribinieri were outside. The Caribinieri, are military police attired in smart uniforms. They are in attendance at important events because there is so much corruption amongst the ordinary police.

On this occasion, all the Caribinieri were gathered round a rare female Caribinieri. She was wearing full dress uniform of breastplate, sword, riding boots and spurs. She had very long curly hair and was wearing a skirt which barely covered her bottom.

South Africa, Johannesburg Airport—
The Differing Bag Count

When the airport automated the car park exit barrier, the person taking the tickets was replaced by a machine. He did not give up, but stayed by the barrier.

He gave everybody their tickets from the automatic machine and was given the money to put in the machine along with a tip. When someone wished to exit, he would then put the ticket in the automatic machine for them, thus releasing the arm.

Johannesburg was one of the few airports where British Airways put their own screening in place before baggage check in. I was intrigued by this and asked why. The surprising answer was pointed out to me, "Just look at the attendants at the hand baggage security screening." Sure enough, there were eight people looking after the security screen, but all of them were profoundly asleep. On the way through to the plane, there was only one man in the departure hall, and he happened to be weeping. I felt badly for him, so asked what was wrong. He indicated he had been late checking in, so he was flying Alitalia.

I'm not sure what he meant, because I found Alitalia on the short haul okay. That is, apart from the stewardesses being a safety hazard in their four—to six-inch heels, and the smutty film, involving a man with a sandwich roll which squirted tomato sauce sideways, and various unsuspecting girls in tight T-shirts sitting on park benches.

Anyway, I boarded my flight, a BA Jumbo, which was absolutely full of people with lots of luggage. It proceeded to taxi slowly through an electrical storm to the beginning of the runway. The pilot then announced there would be a further delay caused by the fact that, already three quarters of an hour after our official take off time, the airport had just reported the plane's two baggage counters had disagreed over the number of bags loaded.

At that point, we should have been over the Botswana desert, but instead, we taxied back to the terminal and the airport authorities removed over five hundred bags and re-checked them. Fortunately, they finished in time for our take off to proceed just before the storm strengthened and the airport was closed. They were finally in agreement about the number of bags.

The more alarming side of South Africa is illustrated by the sad fate of a very tall lady from Uganda. Not only was she an absolutely brilliant fund manager for Barclays, but an actual Ugandan princess as well. Being so tall, she was accidentally shot in a random drive-by shooting in Johannesburg.

The United States—Really Aggressive Airport Security Every Time

Last but not least, I'm not sure I like the United States because the security guards who patrol around the personal baggage scan are seemingly drawn from an underclass of mental and physical bullies. An American friend says he doesn't know here they come from, but there are a few over here in the UK as well.

On one occasion, shortly after a knee replacement, and still disabled, I was made to stand in Heathrow for ten minutes without my walking stick.

The stupidest incident was in Charleston, South Carolina. It is a wonderful town, with Georgian architecture, and it reminds me of a larger version of Leamington Spa in England. I had given a pensions lecture there. However, the airport showed all the prejudice of the US against foreigners. It would do US sycophants, like William Hague, our Foreign Secretary, a world of good to visit the place. As I was returning to the UK via Chicago that day, United Airlines decided I was a high risk terrorist because I was going abroad. They duly stamped three S's (for security risk) on my boarding pass.

The next stage was for me to stand still for nearly half an hour while an employee gave my bag fifty-seven drug swabs very slowly, and so it went on. When I eventually got to the departure lounge, two South Carolina police cycled in, wearing shorts and Stetsons. I was sure that was it for me, however, they arrived for the other passenger in the lounge. Based on my experience, after they took him away, they probably shot him.

Most Colourful Chef

One day I was walking by the Harvey Nichols store in London. I noticed there was a commotion at the Hyde Park Hotel opposite, now the Mandarin Oriental. A sous chef emerged, running for his life, pursued by what looked like Marco Pierre White, waving a cleaver.

There was also a big anti-nuclear demonstration outside the French Embassy next door. The demonstrators recognised the chef event was serious, and the crowd parted like the Red Sea. Unfortunately, because of the crowd's manoeuvres, I didn't see what happened, but the sous chef had the advantage in that he was younger. I wonder what he did—cook the steaks properly so they didn't ooze blood?

Legend has it that Jean Christophe Novelli, during the time he was ensconced at a hotel in Hertfordshire, and after his restaurant in the City went bust, was introduced to two AA restaurant inspectors. Unfortunately, they had just given his new restaurant a nil rating for change of chef and Novelli was incredibly angry at this. He took the view they should know his cooking. He also totally disapproved of the AA guide for rating things other than the cooking. So, he proceeded to yell at them in pretty colourful language, giving forth on his opinions of giving free meals for food critics and what he thought about the AA guide and their review. He then angrily informed them he was throwing them out. They quickly got to their feet and made for the door. But Novelli still had one more thing to say, "Not that way! Get out through the backdoor, like the dogs you are!"

Work

My First Job Obtained by Thinking on my Feet

It turned out the investment department of Guardian Assurance was expanding. Uniquely amongst insurance company investment managers, Guardian's Investment Manager, Norman Shepherd, did not want his staff to be actuaries. I never found out the reason for this, but was pleased he did not.

During the interview, he asked the obvious question, "Do you read the city financial page of your newspaper?" The answer to that was no, so instead I replied, "Didn't you know I replied to your advertisement in the Financial Times?"

Subsequently, it emerged that they had also advertised in the Daily Telegraph. Personnel had told Mr Shepherd that sixteen individuals had replied to the Daily Telegraph, but they had failed to mention that there had also been one reply to the Financial Times advertisement. So I got the job, never revealing it was the first and only occasion I had ever read the Financial Times.

I don't think much has changed since then within many personnel departments, apart from changing their name to Human Resources and adding highfaluting titles and highfaluting pay.

The City in the 60s—No Technology but a Place for Gentlemen

My first job was to learn statistics. Paradoxically, this was helped by being in the pre-electronic calculator age. Calculating was done by approximation with a slide rule. There were also look up tables for common calculations, and hand crank mechanical calculators when detailed numbers were needed.

The fixed interest bond manager was the key investment person for any life assurance company. He was allowed a moustache and an electromechanical calculator. He had to calculate gross redemption yield, which was the normal yield-like shares, plus the appropriate proportion of the appreciation or depreciation to the issue price at which the government would buy it back at a known date. This resulted in the surreal sight of this person setting his mechanical calculator with the necessary formulae, then going out for the normal two-hour lunch, during which the electromechanical calculator would whizz and bang along, giving its answer usually as he stepped back into the office.

This was no problem, since the price normally hadn't moved in that time (compare that with today). The real profits depended on how much commission you paid to the government broker. This determined what position you had on his telephone call list after he had met the government jobber at the Bank of England to discuss supply and demand for the day.

Bearer Shares

A most amusing incident involved a big purchase of shares of the Dutch company Phillips. The man in charge of registering ownership always kept the stack of share certificates on his desk until all the purchase had been delivered to him. He would then register the transfer and deposit the new certificate in the bank.

The purchase of Phillips cost half million pounds. It took six months for all the share certificates to be delivered, so they accumulated on the man in charge's desk. It was only when he had finally sent them to the bank, that we told him Phillips was a Dutch company.

"What does that mean," he enquired. We explained that Dutch shares are *bearer* rather than *registered*, as British or American shares are. This means whoever has possession, owns them. We further explained, "You have had up to the equivalent of half a million pounds cash sitting on your desk for six months! You could have taken them and retired to the South Seas." This would be equivalent to about £50 million in today's money. He was not best pleased.

Working Conditions or Shades of Reginald Perrin (From the TV Series)

In those days, the bowler hat had just disappeared under the fashion influence of President Kennedy. However, we still had to come to the office on Saturday mornings. As a concession, we were allowed to wear sports jackets, but naturally, with a white shirt and tie. We had to start work before nine, and sign in using blue ink. If we arrived after nine, but before nine-thirty, we signed using red ink. If arrival occurred after nine-thirty, we were marked absent. However, the Investment Manager's train always got stuck at Effingham Junction (shades of the TV series *The Rise and Fall of Reginald Perrin*), so he didn't normally arrive before nine-thirty, himself.

Stockbroking as it Was

One day I was having lunch with a friend at a restaurant in the City. To my surprise, I saw the gregarious Great White Gnome, a very well known City of London trader, having lunch on his own.

I asked him, "Are you on your own? Would you like to join us?"

He replied, "No fanks. I eats here early every day. Then I pays me bill and wait for the punters to come in for lunch. I listens to them discuss their inside information about what's going on. When they are about to go, because I've paid me bill, I can nip out to me office just round the corner and deal before they've got back."

Top of the Pile

The Prudential Investment Department in the Early 1970s and Their Coat of Arms

In its glory days, I actually visited the chief investment officer of the Prudential in the massive gothic building near Chancery Lane. According to people's political convictions, this was either like an Oxbridge College, with a quadrangle complete with bicycle racks; or, alternatively, every brick was made with the blood of the workers. There was an enormous pyramid of investment staff, starting with non-operational junior analysts. Amazingly, all of these people were actuaries.

When we were finally shown to the investment manager, we were interrupted by a knock on the door. It was opened by a butler, escorting four maids, one for each person at the meeting. Each maid had a tray, with a cloth, bearing a teapot, milk jug, cup and saucer, spoon, and a plate, all of which bore the Prudential coat of arms. The ultimate mark of status for the investment manager, as a main board director, was that the plates each bore a wrapped chocolate Tunnock's Teacake, a chocolate marshmallow cake, rather than a digestive biscuit.

The Old Ways of Keeping Disasters Quiet.

Informal Regulations Were Much Better.

And, Why the Public Didn't Notice the 1974 Crash When Capitalism Nearly Ended in England.

In those days, it was considered a virtue to keep things quiet, which was commendable. During the meltdown in 1974, then-Prime Minister Harold Wilson, was so left wing that he was accused (in the book *Spycatcher*) of being a member of the Russian KGB. This accusation was so credible that the book was banned. The 1974 crash in England was far worse than the meltdown of 2008.

In 1974, near hyperinflation in prices and costs, together with a taxation system that did not recognise inflation, was putting Britain near the end of capitalism. The first major company to become bankrupt was Rolls Royce. It took a long time to build an aero engine. Meanwhile, the tax law said that the hyperinflationary rise in the cost of raw materials was taxable, meaning companies could not afford new materials when that increase was more than 20 per cent per annum.

There were also rumours that National Westminster Bank was in trouble. It had lent massively on property in order to enable the rash of new high-rise office blocks to be built. However, this was done on floating interest rate mortgages. When interest rates rose, and the relevant building was not yet complete with tenants paying the rent, the developers had nothing to pay the hugely increased interest charges on the overdrafts. Subsequently, they went bankrupt.

In addition, there were still bad debt problems from South America. Lloyds even had a subsidiary Lloyds and BOLSA (Bank of London and South America). In short, there was a banking crisis worse than the recent one.

The handling of the crisis couldn't have been more different. The then-Governor of the Bank of England, Gordon Richardson, formerly chairman of the merchant bank Schroders, called the Chairmen of the four clearing banks—Barclays, Lloyds, National Westminster (now Royal Bank of Scotland), and Midland (now HSBC)—into his office.

His address went something like this: "We understand you are all bankrupt, or near bankrupt. What you will do is not tell anybody there is a crisis, since we must retain the confidence of the man in the street. You will then write off a tenth of your losses in each of the next ten years calling it 'general provisions.' At the end of a decade there will be no crisis, and there will be no panic since nobody will know. If you do not do this, I will cancel your banking licences."

It worked, brilliantly. The man in the street was not even aware there was a crisis.

Nowadays, the merits of silence seem to have been forgotten by our regulators. Indeed it was the regulators because of the rulebook they invented themselves, who first broke news of the crisis with the state of Northern Rock.

Old-Fashioned Fund Management and

Long Alcoholic Lunches

In the early 1980s I was working for the fund management arm of a clearing bank. It was eventually closed down because it didn't make a great deal of money. However, it didn't lose lots of money either. In those days, there was no sign of the simpletons who lose billions because they don't understand that risk is evenly distributed. You will find that if you call heads or tails when it has turned up heads a hundred times, the odds on tails on the next spin will still be even. If all of these arrogant people were fired, there wouldn't be a problem with banks losing money

In the 1980s there were still a few who did things the old way. One colleague went out to lunch every day, using the same approach to alcohol as Winston Churchill. My colleague consumed a couple of bottles of claret at lunchtime, with brandy afterwards, and gin and tonic before. This was rather less than Churchill, but Churchill was supposed to be floating on another plane during his peacetime premiership.

My colleague eventually came back to the office, tried and failed to light a huge cigar, and leant backwards, overturning his chair in the process. He scrambled up, sat down, and rang his other friends to tell them what he had found out over lunch. He thought he was whispering, but the influence of alcohol meant he was speaking loudly. If the idea was any good, the rest of us would have had the opportunity to deal before he had finished talking to his friends.

The Short Platform—The Really Drunk Are Truly Physically Relaxed

One of his friends lived in London during the week, but moved to the country to be with his family at the weekend.

One Friday, the two had been having lunch together, and had consumed quite a lot of alcohol. They then repaired to the pub at Kings Cross Station. After some more alcohol, the friend got onto the last carriage of the eight-car train to Lincolnshire, which was first class. He took off his coat, and left his umbrella and briefcase. He walked forward to the restaurant car and got stuck into the miniature gins for a couple of hours.

In those days, the train compartments had individual doors on the side opposite the corridor to get out. By the time his station approached, he was on autopilot. He went to the back of the train, and put on his coat and exited the train at Market Raisen Station. The only thing he had forgotten was that the train was eight carriages long, and the platform was only four carriages long. Only the first four carriages stopped at the platform. He was in car number eight, and should have gone to the front of the train to get off.

He also didn't know that his wife, concerned about the state he might be in, had decided to go to the station to see for herself. Consequently, she was standing on the platform when the train arrived. She was rewarded by the sight of her husband opening a door four carriages from the platform. He stepped out oblivious and, like the truly drunk usually do, landed softly after taking the fifteen foot drop to the track. He walked along the track ballast to the platform, noticed his wife when he was a couple of feet away from her, and said, "Hello dear, nice of you to come."

Investment in France Is Still Old-Fashioned

In both the UK and the US, the regulators go berserk if they discover there's been insider trading. This is when an investor deals on private information. In the US, where their approach to crime and punishment is draconian (unless you kill someone with a gun), they take a particularly vicious approach to insider trading. Prosecutions are rare in the UK, but in the US, there will be a custodial sentence. They even imprisoned the legendary lifestyle guru, Martha Stewart for insider trading.

The French have a different attitude. There was a prospective takeover of a small life company I worked for by a big French life company. The takeover never happened. However, I went to visit the investment manager of the French company and I explained what my job entailed. I bought shares and bonds in big companies. I then enquired as to what his job entailed, and he replied, "We buy property."

I asked if the property was located in Brittany and Normandy (where most of their policyholders lived) and he replied, "No. We have a non-executive director and his name is Jacques Chirac. He was the mayor of Paris before he became the French President. He has special knowledge of the good areas of Paris which will be released by the municipality of Paris. As he is a non-executive director, it is his duty to tell us first when any sites are going to be released."

Spain

I first visited Spain under Franco. During my trip, I saw a van parked on a double yellow line with an angry civil guard in his tricorn hat hammering on the van with the butt of his revolver.

I genuinely thought the Spanish word for lift was *non functionar* because that notice was on all lifts.

The Generalissimo Franco

At the time of the Falklands War, my boss, Peter, was married to a Spanish lady whose father had been one of Franco's Generals.

After the war, the General said, "Thank goodness you fight in the Malvinas and win."

Peter replied, "Is there any special reason, as a Spaniard, that you would say that?"

The General said, "Because for many years I tell Franco if we invade Gibraltar, you fight and you win."

One favourite saying of the Generalissimo's was apparently, "Do not be concerned about your problems, they will all eventually float down the river in front of you."

The current government of Spain, which has revived the threats against Gibraltar, which is legally British territory, would do well to remember the Generalissimo Franco story above. On the other hand, they may be taking a deliberate gamble on the total lack of backbone of the current British Foreign Secretary, William Jello. All he cares about is grovelling to President Obama. After Obama had spent a week after the gulf oil spill being exceptionally nasty about "British Petroleum", because the CIA didn't realised its name had been "BP" for years, he was actually damaging British trade with the US. Enter William Jello, who said on TV it was quite wrong Obama had been rude about anything British.

David Cameron, can be Jello like himself, withdrawing the plan to stop the grossly abused tax relief for charities because of criticism from the charities—what did he expect? Go and find an MP with moral fibre to be foreign secretary and stand up the the Spanish, who are threatening Gibraltar, which is British Sovereign territory. Usually, as per Margaret Thatcher, moral fibre is easier to find in lady MP's.

The Only Banker who Understood Modern Risks

The only banker recently who really understood the limited intellectual capacity of bankers was Sir Brian Pitman, first CEO, then Chairman, of Lloyds Bank from 1988 to 2001.

I listened to his first talk to investors.

He said, "I am a banker. That is to say, like all bankers, I am not very bright, and have a limited range of understanding. That means I will not invest in things I do not understand, and I don't understand much. Therefore, we will do little or nothing abroad. The last time we did was with the long-since shut Bank of London and South America. This subsidiary cost us a fortune. We will also have nothing to do with investment banking, stockbroking, or derivatives."

How right he was. Lloyds went into this meltdown as one of the world's strongest banks. Unfortunately, he had retired by then, and his successor threw it all away on one conversation with Gordon Brown, when Lloyds bought Halifax Bank of Scotland, which happened to be bankrupt.

However, it may be that the spirit of the old Lloyds Bank lives on in some people trained by Brian. Look how fast they have sorted out the problems they inherited with the Bank of Scotland. In particular, how comparatively slow Royal Bank of Scotland is being at sorting out its losses.

ABN AMRO

One of the few other European banks which had been a pillar of stability was ABN AMRO—Algemene (General) Bank of the Netherlands, Amsterdam and Rotterdam Bank. This was the biggest Dutch Bank—indeed, it was the successor to the legendary Nederlands Mattsheppei—the Dutch East India Company. The ABN, before the merger, brought a long-standing international network, and AMRO a big Dutch branch network. The bank was very sound, but naturally at a time of speculation, its profits growth lagged its international rivals.

New Chairman with a Very High Opinion of Himself and Huge Ignorance, Who Wrecked a Solid Bank

The Managing Board installed Rijkman Groenick as Chair of ABN AMRO. Very unusually for a Dutchman he had strident views, and was not a committee person. As so often happens with that type of person, his views were based on ignorance.

In managing a Bank in over one hundred countries he only had experience of Dutch domestic banking. He did not understand overseas. There was ownership of the world's fastest growing life company in Hungary. I guess the salesmen made sure they were out selling all the time, as the head office was in a former Russian barracks, rumoured to be radioactive.

The sale value (embedded value) of this company, which had only been going about three years, was over £50m. This was the total of the policy premium less commission to salesmen expected over the lifetime of the policies, discounted back for inflation.

However, Groenick talked to the ignorant banking accountants, who only saw the current year, which was making an accounting loss due to paying commission on growing amounts of new business. He paid another bank to take away this embedded value. Worse than that, he found the repeat business of global fund management and life assurance boring, and investment banking exciting. Unfortunately, as a relative new entrant to investment banking, ABN usually got the worst part of any deal, which they were to find out at the crash.

Fred the Shred of RBS Compounds the Problem

Meanwhile, Fred Goodwin, aka, "Fred the Shred" (so named because of how fast he had collapsed costs when he took over NatWest at Royal Bank of Scotland), wanted to buy the very solid US retail bank of la Salle from ABN. It consisted of huge numbers of branches in the conservative mid-west. I once asked to cash a traveller's cheque at the head office branch of la Salle in Chicago, and nobody had even heard of them.

Groenick sold the mid-west bank to Amex as a spoiling move. Instead of admitting defeat, Fred ended up with a bust investment bank together with an international network he did not understand. The clever Dutch had got the British to pay for one of the biggest banking disasters of all time, and the cause of the disaster walked away with £10m for himself.

Well, that's the end of these ramblings, and what I remember of incidents. I hope you liked some of them.

© Copyright 2013 Gregory Randall

Lightning Source UK Ltd.
Milton Keynes UK
UKOW04n0221260913

217935UK00002B/34/P